HEALTHCARE
PAYMENT SYSTEMS

An Introduction

HEALTHCARE
PAYMENT SYSTEMS

An Introduction

DUANE C. ABBEY

CRC Press
Taylor & Francis Group
Boca Raton   London   New York

CRC Press is an imprint of the
Taylor & Francis Group, an **informa** business

A PRODUCTIVITY PRESS BOOK

Productivity Press
Taylor & Francis Group
270 Madison Avenue
New York, NY 10016

© 2009 by Taylor & Francis Group, LLC
Productivity Press is an imprint of Taylor & Francis Group, an Informa business

No claim to original U.S. Government works
Printed in the United States of America on acid-free paper
10 9 8 7 6 5 4 3 2 1

International Standard Book Number-13: 978-1-4200-9277-6 (Softcover)

Library of Congress Cataloging-in-Publication Data

Abbey, Duane C.
  Healthcare payment systems : an introduction / Duane C. Abbey.
       p. ; cm.
  Includes bibliographical references and index.
  ISBN 978-1-4200-9277-6 (papercover : alk. paper)
  1. Medical fees. 2. Health insurance claims. I. Title.
  [DNLM: 1. Fees and Charges--United States. 2. Forms and Records Control--United States. 3.
Insurance, Health, Reimbursement--United States. W 74 AA1 A124h 2009]

  R728.5.A253 2009
  368.38'2--dc22   2009003731

Visit the Taylor & Francis Web site at
http://www.taylorandfrancis.com

and the Productivity Press Web site at
http://www.productivitypress.com

Table of Contents

---

* CPT is a registered trademark of the American Medical Association.

Acknowledgments

The editorial and production staff at Taylor & Francis deserves special attention for their patience and suggestions in the development of this introductory text. In particular, the encouragement of Kristine Mednansky is particularly appreciated.

This book is dedicated to the thousands of students who have participated in Dr. Abbey's workshops over the last two decades. Although questions abound, there are not always answers. Healthcare payment systems represent a challenge and an opportunity. It seems that some opportunities may be insurmountable. Students should always be patient with themselves when delving into the complexities of healthcare payment systems. There are always exceptions, and then exceptions to the exceptions.

Chapter 1

Healthcare Providers

Introduction

To understand healthcare payment systems, you must know about the different types of healthcare providers. With a moment's thought you can probably list a dozen different types of organizations that provide some form of healthcare. The most common are hospitals and clinics. Your community may also have ambulatory surgical centers, rehabilitation centers, home health services, skilled nursing facilities, sports medicine centers, osteopathic clinics, chiropractic clinics, and the like. There can be some commonality for payment mechanisms for the different types of healthcare providers; for instance, patients can pay cash before or at the time of service. However, certain types of payment systems tend to be used more within certain categories of healthcare providers. For example, physicians and clinics tend to be paid based on fee schedules. Hospitals, at least for certain services, are paid through prospective payment processes.

The Medicare program requires the most formal structuring for healthcare providers. Medicare requires certain rules, regulations, conditions of participation, conditions for payment, and approved services. Many of these same conditions carry over to some extent to the various Medicaid programs. For the many private third-party payers, the organizational requirements and types of services may be more relaxed with general healthcare provision limitations imposed at the state level. Most states have rather extensive scope-of-practice laws for many different types of healthcare providers at the level of an individual person. State laws can also extend to licensing and accreditation of various types of healthcare facilities.

Additionally, there is also the standard business organizational structuring, such as the sole proprietorship, partnership, joint ventures, limited liability companies, and various types of corporations, and the list can go on. These business structures are primarily for accounting and tax purposes. Thus we will address these business organizational issues only in passing because the business organization, per se, does not generally affect the healthcare payment mechanisms. However, the business organization can affect who receives payments and how those payments are categorized.

We will discuss different healthcare providers, the general ways in which service providers are organized, and then recognize that many of the more fundamental organizational structures can be combined. Today we have integrated delivery systems that are regional and sometimes national in scope.

Categorizing Healthcare Providers

Studying healthcare payment and payment systems is a technical area involving a great deal of terminology, jargon, and almost endless acronyms. The first term that we need to address in this chapter is the word *provider*. In general, this term refers to an individual or organization that provides healthcare services. This is the way this word is used in most settings. However, if we turn our attention to the Medicare program and specifically look at what is called the Conditions for Payment, or CfPs, this general use of the term *provider* suddenly breaks down.

The CfPs are found in the *Code of Federal Regulations* (CFR), specifically 42 CFR §424. This CFR entry provides the requirements in order to be paid by Medicare and includes information on the process for enrolling in the Medicare program through the use of various CMS-855 forms. In this section, Medicare distinguishes between provider and supplier. Generally, a provider is an organizational entity that has a provider agreement with the Medicare program. The most typical example is a hospital. A supplier is basically anything else that provides healthcare services or healthcare items for which there is no provider agreement as such. This includes a wide range such as physicians, DME supplier, ambulatory surgical centers, and the like. Clearly this distinction between provider and supplier is esoteric; we do not normally think in these terms and this distinction. However, when you read the CFR entries and read legislation from Congress, you will see this distinction made.

We will look very briefly at several typical types of healthcare providers using mainly the Medicare program classification. Our perspective is that of payment systems and payment mechanisms.

Hospitals—Inpatient

There are several thousand hospitals around the country. Hospitals provide inpatient services as well as outpatient services. An inpatient is typically an individual who has been admitted to the hospital by a qualified practitioner for inpatient services. Thus, inpatient services are associated with a length of stay or episode of care, which can vary from less than a day to months and sometimes years. In general the payment systems for hospital inpatient services have been developed based on the length-of-stay concept. This can take the form of a case rate that is based on the severity of illness or sophistication of services. Another approach is to pay for services on a per diem or per day approach, often differentiating surgical services from medical services. We will also discuss some additional payment approaches.

The term *hospital* can have different meanings, particularly in terms of payment processes. In general, hospitals, along with other healthcare providers, are licensed by the individual states. Additionally, certain third-party payers may recognize special designations for certain types of hospitals. These designations often involve increased reimbursement or reimbursement through an alternative payment system.

The Medicare program recognizes certain special situations. When referring to just a hospital, the reference will typically be to a short-term, acute-care hospital. These hospitals, under the Medicare program, are paid through the inpatient prospective payment system Diagnosis-Related Groups, or DRGs.[*] There is a slightly different version of DRGs for Long-Term Care Hospitals, or LTCHs. Medicare also recognizes certain rural, small hospitals as Critical Access Hospitals, or CAHs. These hospitals are cost-based reimbursed and are not covered by the rules and regulations surrounding DRGs.[†]

Additionally, Medicare also recognizes the following specially designated hospitals:

---

[*] The DRG system has recently experienced a major revision and may be referred to as MS-DRGs, or Medicare Severity DRGs. We will use the general acronym DRG to refer to a multitude of DRG-type payment systems.

[†] For instance, CAHs are not subject to the DRG Pre-Admission Window.

■ Sole Community Hospitals (SCHs)
■ Medicare Dependent Hospitals (MDHs)
■ Rural Referral Centers (RRCs)

Each of these special designations provides for increased payment incentives as long as certain criteria are maintained. Thus, there is a base payment system, namely DRGs, along with enhanced payment that is provided through complex formulations.

Add to this discussion the fact that some hospitals are special because of the type of services that are provided. Specialty hospitals have grown in numbers over the years. Additionally, in Chapter 3, where we discuss organizational structuring, we will briefly encounter the concept of a "hospital-within-a-hospital," or HwH.

Note: Great care should be taken to understand that many of these special hospital designations are for the Medicare program. Other third-party payers may or more generally do not recognize these designations. For instance, if a non-Medicare patient goes to a CAH, from the patient's perspective (and the perspective of the patient's insurance company), this is simply a hospital.

Hospitals—Outpatient

Most hospitals provide outpatient care in addition to inpatient services. Over time, the ratio of inpatient to outpatient services has moved more heavily to the outpatient side. So what are outpatient services? This is actually a more difficult question than you might first think. The simplest answer is, "Outpatient services include everything that is not inpatient." Actually, this answer is basically correct. Thus, the range of services provided on an outpatient basis is tremendous. As a result, the payment systems that address hospital outpatient payments have also become complex.

For outpatient services, the process is generally that of an *encounter*. A patient comes to the hospital to receive services, the services are provided, and the patient leaves. The payment for such services typically revolves around the encounter. Generally you will encounter terminology such as the facility payment or the technical component payment. The hospital is receiving payment for resources utilized such as nursing services, rooms, equipment, supplies, and the like.

Outpatient services raise some additional issues. Inpatient services can only be provided in a duly licensed facility that is allowed to provide inpatient services. This is generally inside the hospital in an inpatient bed. What about hospital outpatient services? Where can these services be provided?

Outpatient services can be provided in the hospital itself, but what if we have an outpatient service area that is located outside of the hospital? Perhaps there is an ambulatory care unit that is in a separate building on the campus of the hospital. Or perhaps this unit is several blocks away from the hospital.

Thus, hospitals as outpatient service providers have a wide range of locations and organizational structuring. For the Medicare program, we have the concept of "provider-based" or, if we narrow the provider to a hospital, then the phrase is "hospital-based." We will encounter this concept in Chapter 3.

Hospitals are definitely healthcare providers, generally providing inpatient and outpatient services. Hospitals typically file claims on the UB-04 claim form and the claim is for technical services, that is, facility charges. In contrast, physicians and other qualified practitioners provide services in the hospital setting, both inpatient and outpatient. These services are classified as professional services and the claims filed are generally on the 1500 claim form.

Ambulatory Surgical Centers

Ambulatory Surgical Centers (ASCs) are a special designation developed by the Medicare program. Typically, these are freestanding facilities that provide ambulatory surgeries or surgeries that do not require an extended stay in the hospital. Again, we face a dual definition with ASCs. If a Medicare beneficiary goes to an ASC for surgery, then the ASC must be fully certified under the Medicare program. But what if a non-Medicare patient goes to the same facility for a surgery? For the non-Medicare patient, is this still an ASC? This distinction may seem trivial; however, circumstances do arise that can make this a complicated issue.

The Medicare program has developed a special payment system for ASCs. This payment system is a hybrid of the Medicare Physician Fee Schedule (MPFS) and the Hospital Outpatient Prospective Payment System (HOPPS). Additionally, Medicare has carefully delimited what surgeries can be performed at an ASC and which surgeries must be performed at a hospital on either an outpatient or inpatient basis. If a non-Medicare patient goes to the ASC, do these same Medicare delimitations on what can be performed still apply?

Although the Medicare program has a well-defined payment process for ASCs, what about all of the other private third-party payers? As is so common with healthcare payment, there are enormous variations in how other payers address payment for services in an ASC.

Clinics, Physicians, and Practitioners

Clinics are certainly providers of healthcare services. In many respects, payment issues for clinics revert back to the individual physicians and practitioners who provide services in clinics or medical offices. For our purposes we will separate clinics into two types: freestanding and provider-based.

Freestanding clinics are typically organized and owned by groups of physicians. However, clinics can also be owned and operated by hospitals, in which case the physicians are typically employed or contracted. Provider-based clinics, sometimes called hospital-based clinics, represent a Medicare concept. For a clinic to be provider-based there are several criteria that must be met so that such a clinic is not only owned and operated by the hospital but is also tightly integrated. We will discuss this concept more fully in Chapter 3. For provider-based clinics, Medicare makes technical and professional component payments

To make matters even more complicated, the Medicare program has two additional special types of clinics: Rural Health Clinics (RHCs) and Federally Qualified Health Centers (FQHCs). Both of these special types of clinics have special cost-based payment mechanisms under the Medicare program, and they can also be considered to be freestanding or provider-based depending upon specific circumstances.

The good news for physicians and practitioners, at least for professional payment, is that the most frequent payment system used is a fee schedule. Third-party payers pay the professional charges on the basis of predetermined fees. Of course, there has to be a classification system by which physicians and practitioners can report their services. We shall see that this is the American Medical Association's Current Procedural Terminology (CPT).

Home Health Services

Home Health Agencies (HHAs) represent a Medicare concept. Although many HHAs primarily provide services to the elderly Medicare population, there is certainly a significant portion of services provided to non-Medicare patients. HHAs under the Medicare program must be organized and meet specific standards. For non-Medicare patients, the various standards and requirements generally default to state licensing or certification.

With the baby-boom generation approaching retirement age and thus also Medicare eligibility, home health services is a significant growth area. This same growth will also occur with nursing facility services. As we shall discuss, for Medicare there is a special prospective payment system that is driven by a detailed documentation process.

Independent Diagnostic Testing Facilities

Independent Diagnostic Testing Facilities (IDTFs) are typically physically freestanding operations providing diagnostic testing services, usually radiology services of various types. Although these operations are often owned and operated by groups of physicians, other providers such as hospitals can also develop them. As we mentioned for the provider- or hospital-based clinics, an IDTF owned and operated by a hospital might be able to generate better reimbursement by being part of a hospital. This takes us into the realm of organizational structuring, which we will discuss in Chapter 3.

For the Medicare program, the payment for IDTF services falls to the MPFS. Thus, if you learn about the MPFS, you have also learned about how IDTFs are reimbursed. For private third-party payers, the same approach used for physician payment is often used with IDTFs. Again, there is a split personality because the IDTF is a Medicare concept that may or may not be recognized by other third-party payers.

Comprehensive Outpatient Rehabilitation Facilities

As with several of these special provider types, Comprehensive Outpatient Rehabilitation Facilities (CORFs) again represent a Medicare concept. As the title implies, this is a provider that brings together several different individual service providers including:

▪ Physician/practitioner
▪ Physical therapy/occupational therapy
▪ Speech language pathology

- Respiratory therapy
- Prosthetic and orthotic devices and supplies
- Social
- Psychological services
- Nursing services
- Drugs and biologicals
- Home environment evaluation

From a payment perspective, most of these services can be paid through a fee schedule arrangement. For Medicare this is the MPFS, although the CORF fee schedule is somewhat different. Similarly, other third-party payers tend to pay for these services on a fee schedule arrangement.

Durable Medical Equipment Suppliers

Durable medical equipment (DME) suppliers abound. If you are in a community with a hospital or clinics, then there is certainly going to be someone selling DME even if it is only the corner drugstore. In Chapter 4 we will discuss gaining billing privileges with the Medicare program, which includes the process of becoming a DME supplier. Of course all types of patients may require certain forms of DME such as pillows, canes, walkers, and wheelchairs, to mention just a few.

Because DME can be itemized in detail, the general payment process is to use a fee schedule approach. This means that a given piece of DME will be paid at a given fee schedule amount. There are many ancillary issues that come into play. For instance, some DME must be adjusted, fitted, or even fabricated. The patient must be trained in how to use the DME. Will the DME fee schedule include these costs? Also, just how is the DME to be categorized? For the Medicare program, this has been solved by developing a special set of codes, the E-Codes, which are a part of the CMS Healthcare Common Procedure Coding System (HCPCS). Other private third-party payers may also use this code set to pay for various types of DME.

Note: DME is probably the most heavily monitored area for fraudulent billing and reimbursement under the Medicare program. Thus, there are many safeguards in place to help prevent fraudulent activities in this area. In addition to intended fraudulent activity (i.e., billing for a DME item that was never dispensed) the larger concern is that of medical necessity. For example, when a patient needs a wheelchair, it is all too easy to get one with certain bells and whistles that are not necessary. Of course, this becomes a major payment issue because the payer will pay for the base wheelchair, but the more advanced model needs to be covered by the patient (or secondary payer, if any).

Other Types of Healthcare Providers

We have mentioned just a few healthcare provider types. Developing a truly comprehensive list of different types of healthcare providers and then also considering specialties and a variety of organizational structuring is a difficult task. There are several ways in which to approach this. We will mention two approaches: (1) for the Medicare program, the Provider Type, and (2) the Healthcare Taxonomy Codes.

Medicare Provider Types

Here is a partial listing of the Medicare Provider Types. As we will discuss in Chapter 5, in gaining billing privileges with the Medicare program, an appropriate CMS-855 form must be completed, filed, and approved. These provider types are embedded in the billing privilege process as well as for use in the various Medicare payment systems:

- Rural Referral Center
- Indian Health Service
- Cancer Facility
- Medicare Dependent Hospital
- Medicare Dependent Hospital/Referral Center
- Re-based Sole Community Hospital
- Re-based Sole Community Hospital/Referral Center
- Medical Assistance Facility
- Essential Access Community Hospital
- Essential Access Community Hospital/Referral Center
- Rural Primary Care Hospital
- Hospice
- Home Health Agency
- Critical Access Hospital
- Skilled Nursing Facility
- Hospital-Based ESRD Facility
- Independent ESRD Facility
- Federally Qualified Health Centers

- Religious Non-Medical Healthcare Institutions
- Rural Health Clinics-Free Standing
- Rural Health Clinics-Provider Based
- Comprehensive Outpatient Rehab Facilities
- Community Mental Health Centers
- Outpatient Physical Therapy Services
- Psychiatric Distinct Part
- Rehabilitation Distinct Part
- Short-Term Hospital—Swing Bed
- Long-Term Care Hospital—Swing Bed
- Rehabilitation Facility—Swing Bed
- Critical Access Hospital—Swing Bed
- Rehabilitation Facility—Swing Bed
- Critical Access Hospital—Swing Bed

Even in looking at this list you will see that we could easily add providers such as ASCs or ambulance services.

Healthcare Provider Taxonomy

The taxonomy codes are used in the process of a healthcare provider obtaining a National Provider Identifier (NPI). We will discuss this special type of identifier in Chapters 5 and 6. NPIs have arisen from the Health Insurance Portability and Accountability Act (HIPAA) legislation enacted in 1996.

The provider taxonomy roughly divides providers according to this outline:

- Individual or groups (of individuals)
  - Group
  - Allopathic and Osteopathic Physicians
  - Behavioral Health and Social Service Providers
  - Chiropractic Providers
  - Dental Providers
  - Dietary and Nutritional Service Providers
  - Emergency Medical Service Providers
  - Eye and Vision Services Providers
  - Nursing Service Providers
  - Nursing Service Related Providers

- Other Service Providers
- Pharmacy Service Providers
- Physician Assistants and Advanced Practice Nursing Providers
- Podiatric Medicine and Surgery Service Providers
- Respiratory, Developmental, Rehabilitative and Restorative Service Providers
- Speech, Language, and Hearing Service Providers
- Student, Healthcare
- Technologists, Technicians and Other Technical Service Providers
■ Non-individual
  - Agencies
  - Ambulatory Healthcare Facilities
  - Hospital Units
  - Hospitals
  - Laboratories
  - Managed Care Organizations
  - Nursing and Custodial Care Facilities
  - Residential Treatment Facilities
  - Respite Care Facilities
  - Suppliers
  - Transportation Services

Our intent is to illustrate that there is a significant number of different types of healthcare providers. For payment purposes, each of these types of healthcare providers must be addressed; that is, we need to establish payment systems that can provide payment for services provided. In some cases a single payment system, or type of payment system, can be used with multiple types of providers.

Summary and Conclusion

Even with this brief discussion, you should realize that there are hundreds of different types of providers for healthcare services and/or associated healthcare items. This is a very large industry with many different facets. We will continue our discussions of providers, how they are organized, and particularly how they are paid through a myriad of payment systems. We have already started our payment system discussions in this, the first chapter.

Chapter 2

Chapter 2

Types of Healthcare Payment Systems

Introduction

The number and type of healthcare payment systems are almost beyond comprehension. Even within a broad category of a payment system, there can be dozens if not hundreds of variations. Thus, learning and mastering any given type of payment system must allow for significant degrees of variation and ongoing changes. A general learning approach is to understand the overall type of payment system being considered and then to drill down into specific variable aspects of the given payment system. Furthermore, the actual application and use of the given payment system in a real-world setting can then also be considered.

In the first chapter we concentrated on identifying different types of healthcare providers because the payment systems have been developed to address certain types of services along with different types of providers. As indicated in Chapter 1, there are many different types of healthcare providers both at an individual level and at an organizational level. We will discuss organizational structuring in Chapter 3.

In this chapter we will look at the big picture of healthcare payment systems and processes. For the purposes of this chapter, we will start categorizing different approaches to payment for healthcare services. We will also continue our discussion of concepts and introduce more terminology along with some important fundamental concepts.

To fully learn, master, and keep up to date with a major payment system such as Diagnosis-Related Groups (DRGs), Ambulatory Payment Classifications (APCs), or Resource-Based Relative Value Systems (RBRVS) can consume an individual's entire career. These are all Medicare payment systems that are established statutorily. The updating process is through the *Federal Register*, with thousands of pages annually. Thus, readers are urged to be patient in learning about healthcare payment systems. These are extremely complex systems that require constant study.

Note: In the following discussions, we will first address several different payment systems that are called *fee-for-service* systems. This simply means that payment is made as services are provided. The more services provided, the greater the payment to the healthcare provider. At the very end of this chapter we will discuss *capitated* systems, in which a fixed payment is made in advance and then the healthcare provider provides all necessary services. With capitation, the fewer services provided, the greater the potential for profitability.

Third-Party Payer Concept

Before legal contracts were written in plain language, many contracts involved the use of terms such as *party of the first part* and *party of the second part*, along with recitation as to the relationship of the two (or possibly more) parties. In the fundamental business model for healthcare, an individual goes to a healthcare provider and receives services, and the healthcare provider bills the individual, who then pays for the services. In this model there are two parties: (1) the individual seeking healthcare services, and (2) the healthcare provider rendering services to the individual.

The billing and associated payment processes are quite simple: the provider bills and the individual who received the services then pays. This very fundamental business process is still used today for what are generally termed *self-pay patients*.

Note: There is a very subtle, but important, shift in terminology in the preceding paragraph. The shift involves going from an ***individual*** *seeking healthcare services* to a ***patient*** *who has received healthcare services*. Distinguishing when an individual becomes a patient turns out to be very important. For instance, under the Emergency Medical Treatment and Labor Act (EMTALA), when an individual seeking healthcare services (i.e., possible emergency care) becomes a patient (e.g., admitted to observation), EMTALA no longer applies. The hospital's Conditions of Participation (CoPs) apply.*

Although this two-party model is wonderfully simple, for healthcare payment there is often a third party or sometimes third parties. For instance, a Medicare beneficiary may receive services. Medicare becomes a third party involved in the business arrangements by virtue of making payments. Additionally, there may also be an insurance company that provides supplemental coverage so that there is now an additional third party that can be categorized as a fourth party, although the general usage is to refer to these as secondary payers. Thus, typically, there are third-party payers that can generally be categorized as:

■ Primary
■ Secondary
■ Tertiary

This list can be extended in some cases because circumstances can become convoluted. Identifying all of the possible third-party payers can become difficult.

CASE STUDY 2.1—Minor Automobile Accident

An elderly individual was riding in a vehicle operated by the individual's daughter. An accident with another vehicle occurred and the elderly individual was treated at the hospital.

The facts as presented in the case study are common. Assuming the elderly individual is a Medicare beneficiary, Medicare will be involved as a third-party payer of some sort. However, the first third-party payer will be the daughter's automobile insurance company. This may be in the form of medical payments or liability under the automobile insurance. Thus, Medicare

---

* See EMTALA in the *Code of Federal Regulations* generally at 42 CFR §489.20.

will be secondary and any supplemental coverage will be tertiary. Of course, the situation may be further complicated because the other driver may be held liable, in which case the daughter's insurance would pay but then there would be subrogation to the other driver's insurance.

The phrase *third-party payer* will be used in a very generic sense in this book. *Third-party payer* (TPP) will be used to reference all of the different types of insurance companies and the wide variety of other types of organizations that provide healthcare payment. You may also see the word *carrier* used in a similar sense; some state statutes will use the *carrier* terminology. Also, we may shorten the phrase TPP to simply *payer* and then depend upon the context of the discussion to differentiate a patient as a payer versus an outside entity as a payer.

Note: As is often the case in healthcare, terminology must be carefully delineated. The capitalized term *Carrier* generally refers to the Medicare Part B Medicare Administrative Contractor (MAC); this is the entity that provides physician payment under the Medicare program. The non-capitalized term *carrier* is generic and references all of the different insurance companies or what we will term TPPs.

With the introduction of a third party in the payment process, circumstances can become complicated. Consider the following simple circumstance.

CASE STUDY 2.2—Hospital Services

An individual with insurance coverage needs to have hospital services provided. The insurance company has no contract with the hospital. The services are provided to the individual.

Again, this is a very simple case. When the hospital bills for the services, the bill should actually go to the patient and then the patient will interact with the insurance company, that is, the TPP. However, the hospital, as a courtesy to the patient, most likely will file a claim with the insurance company. The insurance company will pay up to the limits of the insurance policy and then the patient is liable for any remaining payment. If the hospital has a contract with the insurance company, then the hospital will accept whatever the insurance pays (other than deductibles and co-payments) as payment in full.

CASE STUDY 2.3—Hospital Service Additional Payment

A patient who recently received services at the hospital is at the Patient Financial Services office and is complaining that the hospital is overcharging. The individual's insurance has paid a portion of the bill, but the hospital is not under contract with the payer. Thus, there is a remaining balance. This individual is claiming that his insurance has paid for this service and that only the co-payment should be charged.

Case Study 2.3 illustrates the precarious position that healthcare providers encounter when, as a courtesy to their patients, claims are filed to TPPs with whom the healthcare provider has no contract. Because patients have insurance coverage, the patients are likely to believe that everything is paid by the insurance. In cases of this sort, the payer relationship is with the patient, not the healthcare provider.

We will use the TPP concept because of the wide variation in healthcare payment mechanisms. For instance, an individual may be employed at a company that is self-insured; that is, there is simply a fund set up to pay for healthcare services. Also, there can be instances in which pension plans pay for healthcare services. This list of variable entities and organizations that can and do provide for healthcare payment is significant and thus justifies our use of the concept of TPP of any type.

We will now start our discussion of various payment approaches that go beyond simply paying what is charged. In general, TPPs attempt to delimit payments for healthcare services through a variety of mechanisms.

Cost-Based Payment Systems

The first type of payment system is based on costs. Cost-based payment systems simply pay the healthcare provider on the basis of the provider's costs. The really big question with this type of payment system is "What are the healthcare provider's costs?" If there is a way to determine costs, then this process becomes relatively straightforward. Pharmaceutical items are often cost-based reimbursed.

CASE STUDY 2.4—Drug Payment

A private TPP has approached the Apex Medical Center with a contract in which Apex will be paid for all drugs at 10% above the average sales price (ASP). The pharmacy items must be billed with the proper National Drug Code (NDC) and the proper number of units.

Two items of note in Case Study 2.4 are:

1. The cost of the drugs is determined on a standardized data set that is publicly available.
2. There is a classification system, in this case a code set, by which the drugs can be classified including the number of units provided.

Note that Case Study 2.4 addresses only the pharmacy items themselves, not the administration of the drugs.

The example of pharmacy items is relatively limited. What if a payer wanted to use costs as a general basis for reimbursement? The first hurdle that must addressed is to define a way to identify the costs to the healthcare provider. The Medicare program has done this for many years through what is known as the Medicare cost report. This is a very complex form that must be completed by hospitals. Significant concerns arise relative to which costs are acceptable and which are not. Developing the cost report is a very complex and sometimes tedious process.

The second hurdle is to address how much is to be paid. Will the payer reimburse only the costs? Or will there be some sort of percentage increase above the costs? A third hurdle is to determine whether the reimbursement will be on overall costs or if there will be some sort of delineating of healthcare services for which slightly different formulas might be used.

Cost-based reimbursement is on the decline, although there has been a bit of a revival in the Medicare program with Critical Access Hospitals (CAHs). Medicare also pays Rural Health Clinics (RHCs) and Federally Qualified Health Centers (FQHCs) on a cost basis.

Note: Hospitals are still required to file cost reports even though reimbursement to most hospitals is no longer cost based. CMS uses these cost reports as part of a complex process for determining payment for several prospective payment systems (PPSs) such as DRGs (Diagnosis-Related Groups) and APCs (Ambulatory Payment Classifications).

Charge-Based Payment Systems

Charge-based healthcare payment systems are one step removed from cost based. For example, in the hospital setting a fairly typical arrangement is for a payer to pay a percentage of the hospital's charges. For instance, a hospital may have a contract to accept 85% of whatever the hospital charges. Typically there are carve-outs, that is, designated types of service that are paid on a different basis from the main percentage-of-charges contract.

There is a very fundamental assumption in this arrangement. The assumption is that the hospital's charges are uniformly based on their costs. For example, a hospital may have a charge formula of setting charges using a 1.7 multiplier, which means that the charges are 70% greater than cost. Thus, the payer under this type of contract is paying 85% of 170% of costs, or 44.5% above the costs.

This percentage-of-charges concept is relatively straightforward. In practice you will find numerous variations on this theme. Note also that fee schedules and certain PPSs that we will discuss below also use charges as the basis for determining overall payment. However, this use of charges is not direct. Charges are often converted to costs and then complicated statistical studies are used to determine the actual payment.

CASE STUDY 2.5 — Chargemaster Review

The Apex Medical Center has a contract with a TPP that pays 90% of whatever is charged. Although there are some carve-outs, the main payment for inpatient and outpatient services is the 90%. One of the contract provisions is that the TPP can audit Apex's chargemaster every 3 years and there are also strict delimitations on Apex's ability to increase charges on a blanket basis.*

---

* The hospital chargemaster is a listing of all the hospital's charges that are used to bill and generate claims.

A TPP paying on a percentage-of-charges basis will be very sensitive to price increases, pricing of new procedures, drugs, and supply items. The reason this type of payment system is so attractive is the simplicity in the payment arrangement. The hospital and the TPP can easily determine and track payments.

Fee Schedule Payment Systems

Fee schedules abound in healthcare for almost all types of providers. To establish a fee schedule there is one fundamental requirement, namely, a detailed classification system. The classification system is needed to precisely delineate services provided or items rendered. With a classification system the payer can then assign payments to each of the categories in the classification system.

Note: In the following discussion about fee schedule payment systems and PPS we will be referring to several standard code sets. These code sets are more fully discussed in Chapter 6 where we address the HIPAA Transaction Standard/Standard Code Set rule. In the following, we will briefly introduce several code sets along with certain documentation systems that also provide a means of classifying services provided for payment purposes.

For physician services, there is an extensive classification system called Current Procedural Terminology or CPT. There are thousands of CPT codes that describe surgeries, evaluation and management, physical medicine, radiology, and the list goes on. Given this extensive and relatively precise classification system, TPPs can assign payment for each of the CPT codes to establish a payment system.

The best and most extensive example of this type of payment system is Medicare's Resource-Based Relative Value System (RBRVS), which forms the basis for the Medicare Physician Fee Schedule (MPFS). This is an extensive fee schedule that has become fairly complicated over the years. Several additional features have been integrated into this fee schedule. For instance, if a physician performs multiple surgeries (i.e., there are two or more CPT surgical codes), then the procedure paying the most is paid at 100% and the remaining surgeries are paid at 50%. This process of paying less for subsequent services is called *discounting*.

Because payment is attached to each CPT code, a payer, such as Medicare, will become concerned about correct coding and the possibility of upcoding or using inappropriate combinations of codes. Although upcoding (i.e., using an incorrect CPT code to gain more payment) is a compliance issue, inappropriate combinations of codes can be addressed to a certain extent when adjudicating claims. In the case of the Medicare program, a series of edits, actually code combinations not to be used together, has been established. These code combinations are called the National Correct Coding Initiative (NCCI) and currently there are some 200,000 code combinations. The CPT code set does provide for certain modifiers that can be used to circumvent the edits if there is appropriate documentation justifying the use of the codes together.*

We will look more closely at RBRVS in a separate section. Another example of a fee schedule is that used by Medicare to pay for DME, or Durable Medical Equipment. The CPT coding system does not include any classification for DME. Thus, over the years CMS has developed a different coding system called the Healthcare Common Procedure Coding System (HCPCS).† HCPCS is also referred to as Level II for *National*. CMS sometimes refers to HCPCS Level I as CPT. In the past there was also a Level III for *Local* HCPCS codes. In theory, the Level III local codes are no longer used.

Much of the HCPCS coding system addresses supplies, DME, drugs, and a wide range of other items. There are even a few procedure codes. Most of the DME codes start with the letter "E" followed by four digits. Thus you may see the term *E-Codes*.‡ CMS has developed and maintains a fee schedule for DME. Technically, this is the DMEPOS, or DME Prosthetics, Orthotics and Supply fee schedule. A healthcare provider that dispenses DME items can gain billing privileges with Medicare, bill for DME items on the 1500 claim form, and then be paid for the DME presuming medical necessity, physician's order, and other requirements. As you might guess, this fee schedule becomes rather complex because of the many different types of DME, the fact that the DME might be new or used, the DME might be purchased or rented, and the list goes on. The actual payment amounts are calculated and adjusted by CMS on the basis of the costs of such equipment.

---

* Note that certain code combinations can never be used together, whereas others can be used together if appropriate.
† You may also see this referred to as HCFA's Common Procedure Coding System. When the name change from HCFA to CMS occurred, the acronym HCPCS also had to be modified. Luckily, there was an easy fix for the acronym.
‡ As always seems to be the case, there is another area in healthcare coding in which a completely different type of E-Codes appears; this is with ICD-9-CM diagnosis coding in which the E-Codes refer to external cause codes such as for accidents.

Another fee schedule used by the Medicare program is the clinical laboratory fee schedule. CPT has an extensive categorization of laboratory tests. CMS, as well as other payers, can develop payment for these tests on the basis of the costs of performing the tests. Thus, a fixed payment amount for each laboratory test can be established.

As mentioned with the laboratory fee schedules, not only does the Medicare program use fee schedules, but many private payers also use fee schedules. Probably the most common use is with physician payment using CPT codes as the classification mechanism. The actual payment amounts are often determined by a mechanism called the UCR, or usual, customary, and reasonable. The TPP performs statistical studies to determine the payment amounts relative to a geographic area. The TPP will then contract with physicians and clinics and use the contracted fee schedule.

Two issues are often raised with payers use of fee schedules:

1. Exactly how are the payment rates determined?
2. What if the physician or clinic is not contracted by the TPP?

Obtaining the precise statistical processes and data upon which payers determine their fee schedule can be frustrating. Some would use the word *futile*. Although the methods used may not be secret, often this information is not readily available.

The second issue can also be frustrating. If a physician or clinic is not under contract to a given TPP and thus the fee schedule being used, there is no obligation on the part of the physician or clinic to accept the fee schedule payment. Whatever is billed is that which the patient should pay regardless of how much or how little the TPP pays. However, in practice physicians and clinics are in the position that if they do not accept the fee schedule payment only a lawsuit will get them any additional payment.

CASE STUDY 2.6—Worker's Compensation TPP

At the fictitious Acme Medical Center there have been several cases in which injured workers were treated. The worker's compensation insurance company is out of state. In this case the TPP (insurance company) pays on a fixed fee schedule. Thus, only a partial payment has been made and the TPP has indicated that the workers are not to be billed for any additional amounts.

So what should the Acme Medical Clinic do? In theory, there should be a full payment. Is a lawsuit going to yield the additional payment? Is it worth trying to fight this fixed fee schedule approach? These types of questions must be addressed on a case-by-case basis.

Now that we have discussed the basic concepts of fee schedule, let us return to RBRVS, or the Resource-Based Relative Value System that is used by the Medicare program to establish the MPFS, or Medicare Physician Fee Schedule.

RBRVS (Resource-Based Relative Value System)

Covered Services

RBRVS covers a huge range of services that are provided by physicians, practitioners, and certain non-physician providers. The services addressed, in theory, include everything that a physician would perform in almost any setting, including physician offices, clinics, hospitals, surgery centers, and nursing homes, among others. Radiology services are also included. However, laboratory services are included in a separate fee schedule payment process, namely, the clinical laboratory fee schedule. This payment system is for the professional component, that is, the services provided by the physicians and practitioners themselves. In certain cases, the physician may be paid through this system for services provided by subordinate personnel on an incident basis.

Classification System

For RBRVS, and many other fee schedules, the classification system is the same as the coding or data system. For RBRVS, two coding systems are used:

1. CPT, or Current Procedural Terminology: Published by the American Medical Association.
2. HCPCS, or Healthcare Common Procedure Coding System: Published by CMS, the Centers for Medicare and Medicaid Services.

These two coding systems contain thousands of codes for a wide range of procedures. Although RBRVS addresses most CPT codes, there are only select HCPCS codes that involve procedural services. The HCPCS system includes many other types of healthcare supplies, DME, drugs, and the like.

Coding/Data Systems

The same as the classification system.

Relative Value Determination

RBRVS uses relative values or relative value units (RVUs) for each of the codes generating the classification system. In actuality, RBRVS breaks each RVU into three parts, one of which is further subdivided. Here are the components:

1. Work component
2. Practice expense component
   a. Facility practice expense
   b. Non-facility practice expense
3. Medical malpractice

The practice expense component is divided into facility versus non-facility expenses. If a physician or practitioner provides a service in a facility setting, then the facility practice expense component is used. If the physician provides the service in a freestanding or non-facility setting, then the generally higher non-facility practice expense component is used. This difference reflects the fact that the physician has reduced overhead expenses in a facility setting.

For services such as radiology, there are three separate RVUs provided.

1. Total technical and professional
2. Professional component (i.e., Modifier "-26")
3. Technical component (i.e., Modifier "-TC")

The sum of the professional and technical components is the total.

Given the thousands of CPT and HCPCS codes and the fact that the RVU for each code is further subdivided, the overall set of codes and RVUs is quite extensive.* The actual determination of the relative values has been developed through special studies that measure the resource intensity on the part of physicians in providing services.

---

* The entire RBRVS is available for free download from the CMS website in the form of a very large Excel spreadsheet.

Adjudication Process

There are several special features that are discussed below. The Medicare NCCI was originally developed for physician coding and payment. This is a set of approximately 200,000 code combinations not to be used together. If a code pair needs to be used together, then a special modifier is required. Another part of adjudication occurs when a physician provides an evaluation and management (E/M) service along with a procedure. The "-25," Significant Separately Identifiable Service, must be appended to the E/M code for the E/M and the procedure to be paid.

Payment Process—Claim Form

Generally, the 1500 claim form is used to file claims and receive payment under RBRVS. CAHs using Method II reimbursement for physicians and practitioners is an exception in which the UB-04 is used, but the same basic information is used.

Special Features

For Medicare's RBRVS, there are numerous special features that affect the adjudication and, thus, the payment process. Here are a few of the special features:

- Multiple Surgery Discounting: First surgery at 100%, subsequent surgeries at 50%
- Families of Endoscopic Procedures
- Global Surgery Package: Pre-surgery versus intra-surgery versus post-surgery
- Site of Service Differential Payment: See the facility versus non-facility RVUs

Updating Process

RBRVS and most other fee schedules are updated at least annually along with minor quarterly updates. For the MPFS there is the *Federal Register* process in which a proposed set of changes is published in the *Federal Register* and then, after a comment period, CMS issues a final *Federal Register* with all of the changes.

Example

Here is a simple case study.

CASE STUDY 2.7—Lesion Excision

In a physician office setting, a patient with a small lesion may be encountered. The physician examines the patient, investigates the lesion, performs a further integumentary examination to determine there are no other lesions, and then surgically excises the lesion. Luckily, this is a benign lesion that, including margins, measures 1.1 cm in diameter. No suture is required for closure and a dressing is applied.

In this case, we have the E/M service that is separately identifiable from the surgical service. Two different CPT codes will be developed. Although we do not know the exact E/M level (there are five levels, for new patients and established patients), we will assume the E/M is at the second level and the patient is established. The codes and approximate relative values are:

- 99213-25, RVU = 1.70
- 11402, RVU = 3.95

There is no discounting, because there is a single surgery, so that the total RVUs for this visit amount to 5.65. Now we need the conversion factor that we will assume is $40 per RVU so that the final payment is $40 × 5.65, which is $226.

Because a surgery is involved, there is a post-operative period that, in this case, is 10 days. If the patient returns during the postoperative period for surgery related services, the physician has already been paid.

Prospective Payment Systems

Starting in the late 1980s the Medicare program began developing what are termed Prospective Payment Systems (PPSs). The first, and thus oldest PPS is a Diagnosis-Related Group (DRG). DRGs address inpatient services. On the basis of what was perceived to be a highly successful program that curbed inpatient costs for Medicare, additional PPSs have been developed, although development was rather slow until the beginning of the 21st century.

After many delays, the Ambulatory Payment Classification (APC) system was developed for most hospital outpatient services and implemented on August 1, 2000. Interestingly enough, certain outpatient services such as physical and occupation therapy did not go under APCs but were left under the MPFS discussed above.

Other types of healthcare services and providers that now have PPSs under the Medicare program include Skilled Nursing Facilities (SNFs), Home Health Agencies (HHAs), Long-Term Care Hospitals (LTCHs), and Inpatient Rehabilitation Facilities (IRFs). This list seems to be ever increasing.

The general characteristics of any PPS include:

1. Payments are fixed in advance.
2. There is a classification system.
3. Payments are made for categories in the classification system.

Payments or the payment rate for each category is fixed in advance and is usually updated on an annual basis. This can be on a calendar year (i.e., January–December), fiscal year (i.e., October–September),* or any other annual basis. The updating process is called *rebasing* the payments and often involves a conversion factor (CF).

The classification system is the heart of any given PPS. Some classifications are driven by healthcare code sets (e.g., DRGs and APCs), whereas others are much more driven by documentation systems (e.g., SNFs and HHAs). Each category within the classification has a relative weight or relative value. These relative weights are also updated annually through a process called *recalibration.*

The actual payment calculation is generally determined by taking a relative weight that is assigned to each category and then multiplying by the CF. Of course, the CF may also be geographically adjusted through yet another complex statistical process. The geographic adjustment allows higher payment for those healthcare providers that are located in more expensive parts of the country and lower payments for those where the cost of living is lower.

---

* You may see federal fiscal year for the October–September time frame and state fiscal year for the July–June time frame; however, terminology can be variable.

We will now briefly review some of the more common PPSs under the Medicare program. Note that many private payers will piggyback on these Medicare payment mechanisms. In some cases, the TPPs will use the same type of approach whereas in other cases they may modify the given system quite significantly.

Note: The detailed study of any one of these Medicare PPSs can consume a great deal of time and effort. If you specialize in any one of these systems and learn all of the ins and outs and then keep up with all of the changes, you could literally make a career of any one of these PPSs.

Diagnosis-Related Groups (DRGs)

The Medicare program rather suddenly implemented DRGs on October 1, 1984, for FY1985. Up to that point in time, hospitals were cost-based reimbursed for inpatient services. The new DRGs created a significant learning curve for hospitals that lasted for several years. Although a severity refinement was proposed in 1994,* the actual severity refinement was not implemented until October 1, 2007. The new severity refinement is called the Medicare Severity DRG (MS-DRG).

DRGs represent a payment system for hospital inpatient services. Thus, payment is made for a length of stay or an episode of care.

Covered Services

Almost all hospital inpatient services are covered. Note that DRGs address short-term, acute-care hospitals and associated services. There are separate PPSs for specialized hospitals such as LTCHs and IRFs. Also, many other TPPs adopt DRG-type payment systems, often with significant modifications. Thus, coverage may vary significantly depending upon the specific implementation of the DRG payment system being used.

Classification System

The DRG categories represent the classification of services. Although the number of DRGs varies according to the level of refinement, the typical number of categories varies from about 750 on up to 1,500.

---

* This proposed unimplemented system was dubbed as SR-DRGs or Severity Refined DRGs.

Coding/Data Systems

The coding system is ICD-9-CM, using both the diagnosis code set (Volumes 1 and 2) along with the procedure code set (Volume 3). The United States is overdue to move to ICD-10 or possibly ICD-11, both of which represent significant upgrades from ICD-9.

Weight Determination

The relative DRG weights are generally determined through a complex statistical process using claims data. The claims that are filed for inpatient services are grouped to the appropriate DRG categories. The charges associated with the given DRG are then converted to the hospital's cost using the hospital-specific cost-to-charge ratios as derived from the cost report. All of this information is statistically processed to generate the relative DRG weights. A CF (i.e., the dollar amount per DRG weight) is then used to actually generate the payment.

Grouping Process

The grouping process for all DRG-type payment systems is quite complex and is embedded in refined software programs. The code sets used, primarily the ICD-9 code set, and other information from the claim are used to generate a single DRG category for the claim. Note that only one DRG is generated from the grouping process.

Payment Process

The UB-04 claim form is used to file claims for cases under the different DRG payment systems. The claim is grouped to only one DRG category and then the CF is used to generate the final payment amount.

Special Features

There can be many special features depending upon the specific DRG system in use. A fairly common feature is that of *cost outliers*. When there are cases that are unusually expensive, then extra payment may be provided. The opposite is *cost inliers*, in which payment may be reduced if the case is significantly less expensive than anticipated.

There may also be special billing requirements. For instance, with the Medicare DRG system, if certain outpatient services are provided within three dates of service preceding the admission, then some of these services may have to be included with the inpatient service billing. This is known as the DRG Pre-Admission Window. There can also be payment reductions if the length of stay is shorter than the average for a particular DRG category. The CF is generally geographically adjusted. These are just a few of many special features that can be found in various DRG payment systems.

Updating Process

Most DRG systems, including the Medicare DRG system (now the MS-DRG system), are updated annually. The Medicare program updates based on the federal fiscal year, or October 1 through September 30. Through *Federal Register* entries, the National Rulemaking Process (NRMP) involves issuing a proposed set of changes, allowing a comment period, and then issuing a final rule with the changes for the coming fiscal year.

Example

For complex cases involving months in the hospital, the claim involved can literally run into the hundreds of pages and involve charges well over $100,000. Here is a conceptually simple case study.

CASE STUDY 2.8—Inpatient Pneumonia

An elderly patient is admitted through the emergency department (ED) with pneumonia. The patient spends 3 days in the hospital and is discharged home.

The documentation of the case would be reviewed, inpatient-coding staff would code the case, charges would be accumulated, and a claim developed. This is a medical case, so most likely no procedures were performed. The diagnosis codes would drive the specific DRG category. For MS-DRG systems, this would probably group to MS-DRG 195—Simple Pneumonia and Pleurisy—with an approximate weight of 0.7500. If the CF is $5,000, the payment would then be $5,000 × 0.7500, which is $3,750.

Ambulatory Payment Classifications (APCs)

During the early 1990s, the Medicare program funded development of an outpatient PPS that was called APGs, or Ambulatory Patient Groups. Prior research had also been performed on systems such as AVGs, or Ambulatory Visit Groups. Some Medicaid programs and private payers implemented APGs in the mid-to-late 1990s. However, for the Medicare program, final development of their outpatient PPS was delayed until after the turn of the century and was renamed APCs, or Ambulatory Payment Classifications.

The following gives the basic characteristics and methodologies for both APCs and APGs. Note that private payers implementing either APGs or APCs generally make modifications. However, the same general principles will apply even within the modifications.

Covered Services

APCs and APGs are payment systems designed to address hospital outpatient services. The number and type of outpatient services is extremely broad. Often the definition of *outpatient* is given as everything that is *not inpatient*. Obviously, there is no payment system that can cover all healthcare services that are not hospital inpatient. Thus, when working with APCs, APGs, and/or any derivative system, be certain to check first for covered services. For instance, the Medicare APC payment system does not include physical therapy, occupational therapy, and clinical laboratory tests, all of which are paid on separate fee schedule arrangements.

The basis for payment is an *encounter*. The formal definition of an encounter thus becomes critical for these outpatient systems. Generally an encounter is well defined; a patient comes for services, services are provided, and the patient leaves. This is the whole concept of *ambulatory*. However, what if a patient comes to the hospital ED twice in one day for different reasons? Is this part of the same encounter or two different encounters? Although APCs would consider the two visits to the ED to be distinctly different encounters, an APG system might consider this to be part of the same encounter. Again, you must not only understand the general features of the payment system, you must also drill down to understand important variations.

Classification System

APCs or APGs will generally have several hundred different categories. For the Medicare program there are additional categories for special drugs and devices. Each of the categories is designed to represent uniformly consistent services with similar costs involved in the provision of the service that falls within the given category.

As an example, let us consider closed fracture treatment. One way to categorize such treatment is:

1. Closed fracture treatment finger, toe, trunk
2. Closed fracture treatment except finger, toe, trunk

The basic idea is that if a patient presents to the hospital, typically to the ED or an outpatient orthopedic clinic, with a fractured finger, toe, ribs, or the like, then the treatment is relatively minimal and the associated costs of providing services are low.

CASE STUDY 2.9—Fractured Toe

An elderly patient has presented to the Apex Medical Center's ED with a toe injury. The EMTALA-mandated MSE (Medical Screening Examination) is performed and an x-ray of the right foot shows a nondisplaced fracture of the fourth toe. The ED physician instructs the nurse to buddy-tape the toe and prescribes a mild pain medication. No other injuries were noted.

Case Study 2.9 is an example of an encounter in which there is an evaluation and management service (the MSE), then fracture care is provided—in this case buddy-taping the fractured toe along with instructions for care and a pain medication. The fracture care provided is minimal so that the associated payment would also be relatively low.

On the other hand, a patient may present with a displaced fracture of the leg, the ED physician will perform the MSE, x-ray the fractured leg, reduce the fracture, and then apply a cast, if possible. At the very least, after reduction a splint will be applied. This type of fracture care is much more extensive, the costs are greater, and thus there would be higher payment.

Thus, a PPS for hospital outpatient services will tend to have at least these two categories for closed fracture treatment, although there could be more categories if appropriate.

Note: Even in this simple, conceptual example, a given APC- or APG-type payment system may have different payment policies. Two services were provided in each of the above examples: an E/M service and then the fracture care, a surgical service. Some of these systems will pay for both services separately if a modifier is used on the E/M code. Other variations of this type of payment system will bundle the E/M payment into the surgical service (i.e., the fracture care). Another version of such a payment system might bundle minor surgeries into the E/M level.

Coding/Data Systems

APCs, APGs, and variation on these two payment systems use the CPT coding system, the HCPCS coding system, and, in rare cases, may even use the ICD-9-CM diagnosis coding system. Note that CPT and HCPCS are the same coding systems used for physician payment developed through RBRVS. The use of ICD-9-CM codes to drive the determination of a given classification is not common, but these codes may be used to determine E/M levels for services.

Note: Although ICD-9-CM diagnosis codes are used in DRGs to drive the classification, and this code set may also be used on a limited basis for APC- or APG-type payment systems, this code set is always used to establish medical necessity justification for the provision of services or the dispensing of items. Medical necessity is an overarching issue for payment systems.[*] TPPs always insist on paying only for services that are medically necessary.

Documentation is not used, per se, as a mechanism to classify services into one or more of the APC or APG categories. It is the CPT and HCPCS codes along with the various modifiers that drive the grouping process, which then leads to different categories within the classification system.

---

[*] See the RAC (Recovery Audit Contractor) program that is used by Medicare to identify overpayments (and theoretically underpayments). Many of the issues audited under this recovery program involve medical necessity determinations.

Weight Determination

Each APC or APG category has an associated relative weight. The relative weight is designed to reflect the resource intensity consumed by the provision of the service or services that are in the given APC or APG category. Note that these are statistical weights and do not have any monetary value. Thus these weights are relative to each other and cannot be interpreted outside of this limited context.*

The coding systems discussed above are used to generate codes, on the basis of service provided, that are then grouped into one or more APC or APG categories. In the next section we will discuss this grouping process, which can become extremely complex.

For payment purposes, the determination of these weights is all-important. Interestingly enough, for the Medicare program the statistical process that is used to determine the relative weights for APCs is exactly the same statistical process for both DRGs. The basic data that are used analyze the costs for services within a given APC category. Of course, to determine costs, charge data from the claims filed are converted into costs on the basis of the Medicare cost reports for each hospital filing claims. The costs within each category are averaged, the overall costs for all services are averaged, and then a ratio of the average for a given category to the overall average produces the relative weight.†

Grouping Process

The grouping process for APCs and APGs is quite complex. For APCs there is a series of status indicators that help to sort out certain packaging or bundling features. Also, as with RBRVS, multiple surgical procedures are discounted with the highest paying procedure paid at 100% and then subsequent surgical procedures paid at 50%. Modifiers are important in these outpatient PPSs. Generally, there are no global surgical packages, but interrupted surgical procedures must be carefully addressed with appropriate modifiers.

As mentioned above, APCs and APGs are encounter-driven systems. The definition of an encounter can and will vary between different implementa-

---

* Mathematically, these are called "index numbers" because they have no units.
† A special averaging process is used called the *geometric mean*.

tions of these systems. One implementation may use a sliding 3-day window as the definition of an encounter whereas another might be driven by a date of service.

The grouping process for APCs and APGs is quite complex. The biggest difference between these outpatient PPSs and a system like DRGs is that when a case (encounter) is grouped through the APC grouper there may (and most likely will) be more than one APC classification generated. With DRGs, the grouping process generated only one DRG classification.

Payment Process

After a case has been coded, billed, and grouped, then payment can be calculated. The process is to take the different APC or APG categories coming from the grouper, attach the appropriate relative weights, and then multiply by a CF. The CF is generally geographically adjusted. If you review some of the grouping logic discussed above, you will realize that the grouper must be integrated into what is called the *pricer*. The grouper not only groups, but this software also calculates the actual payment. This is necessary to handle features such as multiple procedure discounting and other payment reductions.

Note that with APCs and APGs we rarely concentrate on the relative weights and the CF. For the most part we associate the payment amount with the APC or APG category. The relative weights are still there, as is the CF, but you will primarily see the dollar amounts associated with the APCs or APGs themselves.

Special Features

Delineating special features of APCs or various implementations of APGs represents a very long list. We have already mentioned certain bundling aspects that take different forms. The concept of *significant procedure consolidation* occurs with multiple surgeries that are related so that only the highest paying surgery in a classification is paid. For example, several lacerations might be repaired that would normally group to different classifications, but the grouper may consolidate these related surgeries into just one payment. Similar is the concept of a primary procedure along with supportive procedures. The grouping process is to bundle the supportive procedures into the primary procedure.

Also, we have mentioned the differences in defining what constitutes an encounter. Another area is payment for pharmaceutical items. One system may pay for the drug or vaccine and not pay for the administration. Another system may completely reverse this process. For outpatient PPSs such as APCs and APGs, the number of possible special features is significant.

Example

Outpatient encounters can become quite complicated, such as with observation services spanning several days. In the following case study we will consider a fairly simple ED encounter.

CASE STUDY 2.10—ED Presentation for Fall

An elderly patient presents to the ED after sustaining a fall. There is a laceration on the right arm 3.0 cm in length. The ER physician assesses the patient and orders a chest x-ray and a hematocrit laboratory test. The laceration is repaired with three sutures. The patient is discharged home with family members.

Although the coding can vary based on the specific documentation, let us assume the following coding with some generalized APC categories and payment amounts:

- 99283-25—Level III ED visit, APC = 0614—$140
- 71010—Chest x-ray, APC = 0260—$45
- 85014—Hematocrit, paid under the clinical laboratory fee schedule
- 12002—Laceration repair, APC = 0134—$135

Note that the "-25" modifier has been appended to the Level III ED visit to differentiate it from the other services (x-ray and laceration repair). There is no discounting or other bundling in this case, so that the total payment is the sum of the individual APC payments, that is, $320.

Note that we could have listed the weights for each of the APC categories and then multiplied by the CF. However, when working with APCs or APGs, we tend to associate a payment level with each category.

Home Health Agency PPS and Skilled Nursing Facilities—Resource Utilization Groups

The Medicare PPSs for home health and skilled nursing are relatively new. Also, both of these systems have relatively modest classifications systems that are driven by extensive documentation requirements; thus, there are limited code sets. What we have are extensive forms that must be filled out and then the data basically drive the grouping process. Of course, we still definitely have diagnosis coding using ICD-9-CM and we still have to file claim forms, generally the UB-04.

Home health services have grown rapidly during the last several decades and their growth will probably increase with the baby boom generation maturing. Home health is not only for the elderly, but this is where the bulk of the business occurs. The basic payment unit for home health is a 60-day episode of care. A physician or qualified practitioner must certify and/or recertify the need for the care along with the specific services that generally involve nursing visits and home health aide visits.

Each home health visit must be fully and carefully documented. The initial visit and the more extensive reassessment generate the greatest volume of documentation. The Medicare HHAPPS tends to be quite encompassing, including almost everything that is provided. In theory, the patients under a home health plan of care are homebound except for very specific exceptions. There can be problems generated through payment interfaces. Here is a simple case study.

CASE STUDY 2.11—Home Health after Inpatient Stay

Sarah, an elderly resident of Anywhere, USA, has been in the hospital recovering from an accident. She is being discharged home, where a relative will be looking after her. Unbeknown to the hospital, Sarah's physician decides to order home health services 2 days after her discharge home.

On the surface Case Study 2.11 does not appear to present anything unusual. However, when the Apex Medical Center discharged Sarah, they listed her discharge status as "home." Because the home health services started within 3 days of discharge, the discharge status should have been "home health," and Apex may have received reduced payment under the Medicare DRG payment system.

For SNFs, the basic unit of payment is a per diem rate. Medical necessity along with certification and recertification are all needed. The classification system is called RUGs, for Resource Utilization Groups. For Medicare, SNFs are also subjected to what is called *consolidated billing*. This simply means that when an individual is in a SNF bed, almost all of the services that are provided will be paid by the SNF payment. For instance, SNF patients often require physical therapy. The SNF itself may have physical therapists or physical therapists from a local hospital may be contracted to provide services. The payment for these services is included in the SNF payment.

The specific classification within the RUGs is driven by an extensive documentation system along with diagnosis codes from ICD-9-CM. For SNFs, there is heavy interaction with physician visits and patients to assess, reassess, and make various orders. Documentation processes include:

- Resident Assessment Instrument (RAI)
- Minimum Data Set (MDS)
- Resident Assessment Protocols (RAPs)

Note that SNFs are distinctly different from Nursing Facilities (NFs), Intermediate Care Facilities (ICFs), and Long-Term Care Facilities (LTCFs). For instance, PEN (Parenteral/Enteral Nutrition) Therapy can be provided in SNFs and NFs. For the SNFs these nutritional services are consolidated under the SNF payment that is generally through Medicare Part A. However, for NFs these nutritional services are separately billable under Medicare Part B.

Note also that skilled nursing services may be provided inside a hospital either through a distinct-part SNF unit or through what are called *swing beds*. From a payment system perspective, the really important note is that these two systems are heavily driven by documentation as opposed to coding through extensive code sets as we have discussed with DRGs, APCs, and RBRVS.

Special and Hybrid Payment Systems

To use the term *special* payment systems is redundant. Almost any healthcare payment system is special in one way or another. What we will discuss is a payment system that uses two different payment systems in combination. This is the Medicare payment system for Ambulatory Surgical Centers, or ASCs.

ASCs represent a special classification of healthcare providers under the Medicare program as a general concept of providing less serious outpatient surgeries. Other payers may or may not recognize this specific organizational form for payment purposes. In Chapter 3 we will discuss this organizational structure in the context of several other types of healthcare providers.

ASCs perform a wide range of surgical procedures. Some of these surgeries are classified as physician-office surgeries whereas others are outpatient surgeries that can be performed in an ASC. The Medicare program keeps a list of which surgeries are office-based versus ASC versus other outpatient surgeries that must be performed in a hospital setting. CMS has taken two other payment systems and joined them to make payments for ASC procedures. The two systems are:

1. APCs, the Hospital Outpatient PPS
2. RBRVS, the Medicare Physician Fee Schedule

We have provided an introduction to both of these systems earlier in this chapter. What CMS has done is to develop a formula to pay for ASC services. The formula for the payment for an ASC surgical procedure is the lesser of:

■ 65% of the APC payment, or
■ The non-facility component of the practice-expense RVU from RBRVS

The basic idea behind this formulation is that the overhead expense at an ASC is lower than that at a hospital. So even if the given surgery could be performed in the hospital or the ASC, the ASC will get only 65% of what the hospital would receive. The other part of the formula is to protect any overpayment for minor procedures that could be performed in a physician-office setting. If, per chance, APCs paid more than that paid through the practice-expense portion of the RVU from RBRVS, then the ASC will receive only what a physician would receive for the overhead component of RBRVS.

Note that other payers may or may not recognize the ASC designation. For some other payers, these surgical procedures may be paid as regular hospital procedures are paid. Also, other non-Medicare payers may allow greater latitude in surgical procedures that will be paid when performed in an ASC.

CASE STUDY 2.12—Outpatient Surgery—ASC versus Hospital

Sam, an elderly resident of Anywhere, USA, elects to undergo outpatient surgery. His surgeon indicates that this can be performed at the ASC or at the hospital on an outpatient basis. Sam has a supplemental policy to his primary Medicare coverage.

From Sam's perspective, the decision as to which setting to use is almost purely a quality-of-care issue. Sam will not pay anything regardless of the setting. The Medicare program and the supplemental insurance will pay less if this procedure is performed at the ASC. If Sam were paying his own co-payment amount, then the ASC would be less.

Because of all of the different types of providers and different sites in which the same services can be provided, there are sometimes significant differences in payment for the same service depending upon the site of the service.

Note: In Chapter 3 we will encounter what is termed the *site-of-service differential* when we discuss the difference in payment for a freestanding clinic versus a provider-based clinic. This concept will again involve the APC and RBRVS payment systems.

Capitated Payment Systems

All of the payment systems discussed above can generally be referred to as fee-for-service, or FFS-type payment systems. An individual goes to a healthcare provider, services are rendered, and then the patient and/or a TPP pay for the services performed and/or items rendered on the basis of those specific services. This is why having a classification system is so important. Presuming the patient has insurance coverage of some sort, note that all of the risk associated with the volume and complexity of services rests with the payer involved. The healthcare provider, from a financial standpoint, generates more payment on the basis of the volume and complexity of services. This is why the concept of medical necessity is all-important. A payer does not want to be financially obligated to pay for services that are not medically necessary. This means that the locus or location of risk is with the payer and not with the healthcare provider.

Capitated payment systems are truly a paradigm change. In the capitated model, the healthcare provider is paid a fixed sum of money in advance. The healthcare provider then agrees to provide any needed healthcare services. The capitated payments are often made on a monthly basis. The acronym PMPM stands for per-member-per-month. The TPP in this case knows exactly how much it will pay to cover the services for any covered members of the capitated plan.

Note that the locus of risk has completely changed. The healthcare provider is at risk. If the members in the capitated plan do not need services during a given month, then the money paid is basically profit. However, if there are extensive services provided, then the healthcare provider may lose money for the month. Although this basic concept is fairly simple, actually establishing a capitated plan is quite complex. For instance, primary care physician services, specialty physician services, and hospital inpatient and outpatient services must also be considered. What if the covered member receives services elsewhere and/or what if there are unusual services required?

For our purposes, the general concept of capitation is of importance. Again, note that the location of risk has changed. Now the financial incentive for the healthcare provider is not to provide services (i.e., provide only services that are really necessary). The concern on the part of a TPP sponsoring a capitated plan is that its members do receive the services that are truly needed. In the FFS approach, it is the TPP that is concerned about unnecessary services or experimental services being provided.

CASE STUDY 2.13—Capitated Plan

The Apex Medical Center and the Acme Medical Clinic have been approached about participating in a capitated arrangement for patients in their geographic area. Although several meetings and presentations have been made, the clinic and the hospital have significant reservations about this arrangement and the assumption of risk.

One of the stumbling blocks for healthcare providers is that generally they do not have actuarial information concerning the anticipated incidence of services for a given (and possibly changing) patient population. Private payers, particularly insurance companies, have spent years developing actuarial data and analyses to determine overall risk and anticipated use of services.

Payment System Interfaces

In Chapter 4 we will look at how some of these payment systems interface with each other. A given service might be paid under several different payment systems depending upon circumstances. Let us consider a simple example with the Medicare program.

CASE STUDY 2.14—Coronary Stent Placement

An elderly patient had a diagnostic heart catheterization at a smaller hospital 2 weeks ago. The patient is presenting for percutaneous stent placement. The physician has decided to admit the patient to the hospital as an inpatient. However, utilization review personnel at the hospital think this should be an outpatient procedure.

Assuming that this is a Medicare patient, if the procedure is performed on an inpatient basis, the payment system will be DRGs. If the services are provided on an outpatient basis, the payment system will be APCs. If these two payment systems interface smoothly, there will not be a significant difference in payment. After all, it is the same procedure, using the same equipment, supplies, nurses, and so forth. Even as an outpatient, the individual may stay overnight in extended recovery or observation. As an inpatient there will probably be an overnight stay as well. However, if you look at the payment difference between these two payment systems for the same service, you may be surprised to see the size of the difference.

As we will discuss in Chapter 4, there are many payment system interfaces even if we limit our scope of consideration to just the Medicare payment systems. Often, there are relatively large differences in payment; that is, these payment systems have not been designed to interface smoothly so that there is no real monetary incentive to perform a given service under one payment system versus another.

This then leads to a discussion in Chapter 7 concerning various compliance issues. A major compliance issue is medical necessity. Presuming that a given service is medically necessary, then the question becomes was it necessary to perform the service in a given setting versus another setting in which the payment would have been lower? In Case Study 2.14, this medical necessity issue involves whether or not the stenting procedure really needed to be performed on an inpatient (more expensive) basis versus an outpatient (less expensive) basis. This is an area that is a major focus for the Medicare RAC (Recovery Audit Contractor) audits.

Managed Care and Payment Systems

Throughout this chapter we have been referring to the generic concept of the TPP or payer. The concept of *managed care* is used in a variety of ways. Managed care companies can simply be a TPP or they can become involved in the actual management of healthcare. The dividing line between an insurance company that sponsors healthcare coverage and a managed care company that provides some form of healthcare insurance can be very indistinct.

When you hear references to private contracts with a payer, such contracts may or may not involve some form of healthcare management; however, such contracts invariably address the payment process for the provision of healthcare services for covered individuals under the contract.

As with other examples of healthcare payment systems and processes, we will briefly discuss the Medicare program's approach to managed care. Although the terminology for Medicare managed care continues to evolve, we will discuss the Medicare Advantage programs. As you might guess after reading through the examples above, there are variations within even the Medicare Advantage programs.

Medicare Advantage

The Medicare Advantage programs (i.e., Medicare Part C) represent an example of managed care with capitation overtones. Whether there is truly any management of care may vary. The basic idea is that an insurance company steps in between Medicare and the Medicare beneficiaries relative to payment. The Medicare program pays the insurance company fixed amounts of money and then the insurance company pays for the healthcare services provided to covered Medicare beneficiaries. Obviously, these types of programs can and do become extremely complex.

Although there are variations, a typical Medicare Advantage program will provide for both Part A (hospital) and Part B (physician) services. Hospice is usually carved out. Part D (i.e., drug coverage) may also be included. In a very real sense the insurance company is assuming the risk and also adjudicating claims so that the traditional FFS Medicare claims adjudication is diminished.

The insurance company sponsoring a Medicare Advantage program then goes out and markets the program to the Medicare beneficiaries. From the insurance company's point of view, the most important elements are the negotiation of payment from Medicare and then the marketing of such coverage to Medicare beneficiaries.

All right, we have an insurance company sponsoring a Medicare Advantage program, the insurance company has a contract with the Medicare program, and Medicare beneficiaries are enrolling in the plan. How does this affect healthcare providers and the Medicare beneficiaries themselves?

With many of these Medicare Advantage plans, healthcare providers such as hospitals and physicians, the payment process is based on traditional Medicare approaches such as APCs and RBRVS. For instance, the insurance company sponsoring such a plan might contract with physicians and clinics on the basis that not only will they pay the regular Medicare rate, but also they will pay at 115% of the MPFS. For physicians this can be quite attractive, as would similar enhancements for hospitals or any other healthcare provider. Note that the locus of risk has not passed over to the healthcare provider in this example. The risk is located with the insurance company. From the Medicare beneficiary's point of view, these plans can be quite attractive because the insurance company may well add in benefits that are not included with traditional Medicare.

Note: This is a very brief summary discussion of the Medicare Advantage programs. As with other Medicare payment systems, an entire career can be spent studying and fully understanding this payment system. We have touched very lightly at a conceptual level on a very complex topic.

Other Managed Care Payment Systems

There is a whole set of specialized language, acronyms, and concepts surrounding managed care. Even with the Medicare Advantage programs you will encounter:

■ PPO—Preferred Provider Organization
■ HMO—Health Maintenance Organization
■ MCO—Managed Care Organizations
■ EPOs—Exclusive Provider Organizations

Although our emphasis is on payment systems and associated mechanisms, you will find that payment is sometimes interlaced with medical management concepts. For instance, here are several concepts that you might encounter in studying managed care payment systems:

■ Quality management/quality assurance: The focus on quality has to do with accessibility to proper care that is delivered in a timely manner according to appropriate standards of care. Significant reporting mechanisms with virtually all TPPs have been developed and can now be monitored with standard coding systems that address severity of illness. Some healthcare payment systems provide additional payment just for additional data being reported relative to quality management.
■ Utilization management: Utilization management is an established part of hospital, skilled nursing, and other longer-term healthcare providers. The basic idea is to coordinate and monitor how much care is needed and the cost-effectiveness of such care. Preauthorization is a common technique used to assure proper utilization of sometimes scarce healthcare services.
■ Outcomes management: When a particular condition or disease process is encountered, outcomes management emphasizes the expectation on the part of the patient and providers. In some cases patients do not expect or anticipate full recovery, although the anticipated outcome should be well defined. Managed care payment approaches are very sensitive to providing the absolutely highest technology and most expensive approaches in all cases.
■ Demand management: With many payment systems there is no consideration of the variable demands on the part of patients. Healthcare

providers are at the mercy of patient demands that can and do vary significantly. If a payment system or care management approach can smooth the ups and downs in demand curves, then services can be more economically provided.

■ Disease management: This focus is often a favorite of physicians and clinicians. The specific focus is on specific diseases and/or medical syndromes. Treatment protocols, treatment plans, treatment costs, patient education, and patient monitoring are all brought together under the umbrella of a specific disease or condition.

Summary and Conclusion

We started with the simplest possible healthcare payment process, namely, a patient going to a healthcare provider, requesting services, receiving services, and then paying for those services. This very simple model is still in use today for what are called self-pay patients. A major challenge for this model is the question, "What if the patient cannot pay?" We moved from this simple model that involves two parties and added a third party, namely, a separate payer or a TPP. This can be an insurance company, third-party administrator, a retirement plan, and a host of other entities including various statutorily established programs such as Medicare and Medicaid.

Once we introduce a payer, then we move into the realm of having a payment system of some sort. Of course the payer could just pay whatever the healthcare provider charges. Although this does happen, TPPs have developed very complex, formal payment systems and associated processes to make proper payment for healthcare services.

The oldest of these systems is to pay based on costs, perhaps slightly above costs. Payment based on costs requires that the TPP knows what the providers' costs are. For the Medicare program this involves the rather complicated Medicare cost report. Although the cost report is used in very limited circumstances to directly pay for healthcare services (e.g., CAHs), the cost report is currently used to gather data to accurately convert charges into costs. The cost data are then used in more recent payment systems, namely, the PPSs.

One step beyond cost-based payment systems are charge-based payment systems. Some private TPPs do have contracts by which payment is a fixed percentage; say 85% of the amount charged. In this type of arrangement the payer is presuming that the charges are consistently marked-up above the costs.

In recent years the Medicare program has developed several PPSs. These systems are complex. The main characteristics of these systems are that payment, or at least the payment rate, is fixed in advance and there is a classification system by which services provided can be classified for payment purposes.

Another type of payment system that requires an extensive classification system is the fee schedule. With fee schedule payment systems, the payment that is made to a provider is the lesser of the amount charged or the fee schedule amount. The main fee schedule for the Medicare program is the MPFS, although many providers are also paid through the clinical laboratory fee schedule and the DMEPOS Fee Schedule. Many private payers also use fee schedules of various types. The most common classification systems involve the CPT and HCPCS coding systems.

Over the past 2 decades there has been a different type of payment system developed. This is what is termed *managed care*, although this phrase can have different meanings depending upon the context of discussion. The basic idea is that the TPP introduces the idea of managing the care to hold down costs (i.e., payments for healthcare services). This still presumes what is called a FFS approach in that healthcare payments are made based on the level and intensity of services provided.

Capitation is a paradigm shift from the FFS concept. With capitated payment arrangements, the payer pays a fixed amount in advance and the healthcare provider agrees to provide any and all necessary services. Such arrangements are typically on a per-member-per-month arrangement. This really is a radical change because the location of risk has changed from the payer to the provider. If the provider is receiving a fixed amount and the service levels invoke costs that are above the capitated payment, then the provider will lose money.

The bottom line is that there is a huge spectrum of different types of payment systems. Even if we look at a specific type of payment system, there can be many different implementations made by different TPPs.

Chapter 3

Healthcare Provider Organizational Structuring

Introduction

In Chapter 1 we discussed a relatively long list of different types of healthcare providers. The different types of healthcare providers arise because of different types of services and also as a result of licensing, certification, and designations primarily in relation to the Medicare program. In Chapter 2 we discussed a variety of different types of payment systems that are used to reimburse the wide variety of healthcare providers. In this chapter we will briefly investigate how different types of healthcare providers can come together to form much larger and more diversified healthcare organizations.

Probably the simplest organizational level is a solo physician providing services as a sole proprietor. At the other end of the spectrum is a large-scale integrated delivery system (IDS) that can involve hundreds of hospitals, clinics, home health agencies, skilled nursing facilities, and the like. The business structure for such an enterprise will be significantly more complex. So also will be the payment process for the various types of services provided.

We will look at some representative examples of organizational structuring. Our emphasis is the healthcare payment systems with particular concern about how different types of payment systems for different types of providers come together. The Medicare program payment systems and associated organizational structuring will be the primary basis. Private payers often piggyback on what the Medicare program has done, although major modifications may be made as well as minor modifications depending upon circumstances.

Business Structuring

Even in the introduction for this chapter the concept of business structuring has entered our discussion. Business structuring generally relates to different forms of tax recognition. Healthcare providers in any form are businesses. Thus, there will always be an underlying business structure, tax identification numbers (TINs), financial identification numbers (FINs), employer identification numbers (EINs), Social Security numbers (SSNs), and the like. Specific to healthcare providers are special identifications such as DEA (Drug Enforcement Administration) numbers and NPIs, or National Provider Identifiers.

Although our focus is on healthcare payment systems, business structuring terminology will from time to time enter into our discussions. Here is a short list of business organizational structuring terminology with which you should be familiar:

- Sole proprietor
- Partnership
- Joint venture
- Limited liability company
- Limited liability partnership
- C-corporation, S-corporation, and not-for-profit corporation
- Professional corporation

These business structures are governed by federal tax laws as well as state laws. Thus, you may see slightly modified terminology in different states, but the basic business structures will generally be similar.

If these business structures were always used independently, then life would not be all that complicated. However, in real life, complex organizational structures are developed using these basic structures as building blocks.

CASE STUDY 3.1—Clinic with Independent Practices

You are visiting what appears to be a clinic with five physicians. There is a common encounter point and a common waiting area, and all of the billing and accounting is done by a single set of employees. However, when you probe more deeply you find that the clinic is really a partnership of three professional corporations and two sole proprietors. All of the staff, including nursing staff, are employed by the partnership. The physicians are employed independently by their own businesses or, for the sole proprietors, the physicians are synonymous with their business.

CASE STUDY 3.2—Hospital Clinics and ASC

The Apex Medical Center is a hospital that is organized as a not-for-profit entity. There is an ASC (Ambulatory Surgical Center) on the campus that is a joint venture between the hospital and a partnership of physicians. Apex also owns five medical clinics. Two of the clinics are organized as provider-based; that is, they are considered to be part of the hospital outpatient department. The other three clinics are freestanding clinics, all of which are owned by a separate corporation that is wholly owned by the hospital. Additionally, all of the physicians and practitioners at the freestanding clinics have employment contracts with the hospital from a partnership of the physicians.

With seemingly little effort, complex business and organizational arrangements are developed by a variety of healthcare providers. Sorting out how these complex organizational structures are paid for services under a wide variety of payment systems can become a real challenge. If you find yourself in such a complex organization and/or are called in to assess such organizational structures relative to payment, your first step should be to determine exactly who is what. This may sound trivial, but the names used by different organizations are often quite different from their official legal names through the doing-business-as (DBA) process.

Note: If you are going to be heavily involved in fully understanding healthcare payment systems and the way in which healthcare organizations are paid through these systems, then you will need to take some time to study the different types of business structures that can and are used. Note that there are tax concerns, legal liability concerns, state law restrictions, reporting requirements, licensing requirements, and a host of other issues that involve business structuring. Check for continuing education courses in the accounting and financial planning areas that address business structures.

Freestanding Healthcare Providers

Solo Physician Practice

Probably the simplest organizational structure is with a single provider, typically a physician, operating a solo practice. Although the number of solo physician practices has certainly declined over the years, there are some still in operation. The payment process for such a practice is usually through various fee schedules including the Medicare Physician Fee Schedule (MPFS) for Medicare beneficiaries. Claims are filed on the 1500 claim form using Current Procedural Terminology (CPT) and Healthcare Common Procedure Coding System (HCPCS) codes along with ICD-9-CM diagnosis codes for medical necessity justification.

Because a solo physician practice, or even a freestanding clinic with several physicians, is paid based primarily on different fee schedules, the charges that are made will be at or above the highest paying fee schedule. If the physician did not set charges at least equal to the highest paying fee schedule, then the physician would be losing money. Thus the charge structures for physicians can become somewhat inflated because of this strategy.

Note: We are using the term *freestanding* to indicate that the provider organization being discussed is such that there are no other formally affiliated provider organizations. When we discuss *provider-based clinics* later in this chapter, we will discuss the formal concept of freestanding versus provider-based status under the Medicare program. The formal guidance for this concept is found in the *Code of Federal Regulations* at 42 CFR §413.65. Note also that freestanding is a logical organizational concept, not a physical concept. This means that the freestanding facility can literally be physically inside another provider but there is no organizational connection. For example, our solo physician practice might rent space from a hospital and be physically located inside of the hospital.*

Other Freestanding Healthcare Providers

The same concept of being freestanding can be applied to almost any healthcare provider. For instance a standalone HHA (Home Health Agency),

---

* The revenue code sequences 051X and 052X used on the UB-04 form do not appear to correlate directly to the provider-based logical concept.

SNF (Skilled Nursing Facility), or IDTF (Independent Diagnostic Testing Facility) are freestanding. In each of these examples, there will be a limited range of payment systems that are typically designed for the specific types of services being provided. For HHAs and SNFs, the Medicare program has developed different PPSs. Private TPPs may piggyback on the Medicare approach or they may use other payment mechanisms. However, the payment systems used are designed for the specific types of services provided.

The IDTF payment systems are much more closely aligned with physician fee schedules. Under the Medicare program, the MPFS is used to pay for IDTF services using CPT as the classification system. If you consider IDTF services for non-Medicare patients, then the range of services may expand and a wider variety of payment systems may come into play.

Freestanding ASCs

Another example of a freestanding entity is an ASC, or Ambulatory Surgical Center. As with many healthcare providers, ASCs are really a Medicare concept, although we also use this same name in a broader sense. ASCs appear in different locations and have varying ownership structures and different associations with other healthcare providers. The payment system used for ASCs, at least for the Medicare program, is a hybrid of APCs (the hospital outpatient prospective payment system) and Resource-Based Relative Value Systems (RBRVS) or the MPFS.

Relative to surgical procedures, the Medicare program divides surgical procedures into three different categories:

1. Surgical procedures that can only be performed in a hospital setting, inpatient or outpatient
2. Surgical procedures that can be performed in an ASC
3. Surgical procedures that are physician-office based.

Certainly, surgical procedures that can be performed in a physician's office can be performed in an ASC. These are generally minor surgical procedures such as simple dermatological procedures. However, the more complex surgeries must be performed in a hospital setting.

Note: Although Medicare delimits surgical procedures that can be performed in an ASC, other private TPPs may be more liberal in what services can be provided in an ASC. Thus, the payment systems for private TPPs are more broadly based.

As we discussed in Chapter 2, Medicare payment for ASCs is based on the following formula or algorithm:

1. For regular ASC procedures, 65% of the Ambulatory Payment Classification (APC) payment
2. For office-based procedures the lesser of
   a. 65% of the APC payment, or
   b. The RBRVS payment generated by the non-facility practice expense relative value unit (RVU).

All right, this algorithm becomes a bit convoluted. Let us consider the following case study in which we delve more deeply into this formula.

CASE STUDY 3.3—Office-Based Surgical Procedure Payment

The administrator at the Perigee ASC located in Anywhere, USA, has been asked to analyze whether there are any major differences in payments for office-based procedures. Among the many services are CPT 10080 and 10081, which involve incision and drainage of Pilonidal cysts, simple versus complex. The following chart summarizes the APC and non-facility practice expense payments.

CPT	65% of APC Payment	Non-Facility RVU	ASC (lesser of)
10080	$90	$100	$90
10081	$540	$130	$130

The administrator will need to extend this type of calculation to several other surgical procedures to determine if there are significant differences in payment between their offices and the hospital or the ASC.

Freestanding Hospitals

Hospitals can also be freestanding, that is, not associated with any other healthcare provider. However, even a self-contained hospital will have a fairly wide range of services. Consider a modest-sized community hospital.

CASE STUDY 3.4—Small Community Hospital

The Apex Medical Center is a community hospital located 40 miles from the nearest community with a hospital. Although Apex has not developed an extensive set of services, they do have the following:

- Inpatient services—medical and surgical
- Outpatient services—surgery, observation, infusion, and chemotherapy
- Physical therapy and occupational therapy
- Medical nutrition therapy and diabetes self-management training
- Clinical laboratory
- Radiology services
- Full-service emergency department
- Durable medical equipment

In Case Study 3.4, even with this modest list of services and considering only the Medicare payment systems, Apex comes under a variety of payment systems, including several discussed in Chapter 2, namely Diagnosis-Related Groups (DRGs), APCs, MPFS for physical/occupational therapy, the Clinical Laboratory Fee Schedule, and the DME fee schedule. If you take these services and add in all of the other private payer payment systems that may be in use, Apex may be dealing with a hundred different payment systems.

Provider-Based Facilities

The concept of provider-based facilities is a Medicare concept, although some private payers may also recognize this same organizational structure. Provider-based reimbursement can complicate the payment structure depending upon the specific circumstances. For instance, a hospital, the provider, or main provider may own and operate a Rural Health Clinic (RHC). Certain criteria must be met to have a RHC. Presuming that the criteria are attained, the RHC services for Medicare beneficiaries are paid on a cost basis. The basic mechanism is to make interim payments and then to reconcile the payments to the associated costs.

Now RHCs can be either freestanding or provider-based. If the RHC is not associated with a provider such as a hospital, then the RHC payment process is slightly different in detail, but conceptually the same cost-based reimbursement process is used. Note that RHCs and FQHCs (Federally Qualified Health Centers) are closely related. One of the big differences, in terms of payment, is that there is no co-payment at FQHCs.

Note: Being provider-based is a Medicare concept just as being a Critical Access Hospital (CAH) is a Medicare concept. When a non-Medicare patient comes to an RHC or CAH, the patient is simply coming to a clinic or hospital, respectively. As we will mention, some private payers do recognize these special Medicare designations for payment purposes.

Our main discussion will address provider-based clinics as regulated under the Medicare program. The so-called Provider-Based Rule (PBR) is found in the *Code of Federal Regulations* at 42 CFR §413.65. Although this rule is not particularly long, reading through the regulation can be confusing. The basic idea is that a main provider (e.g., a hospital) organizes a clinic to be part of the hospital, typically the outpatient department. For the clinic to be provider-based, these criteria must be met:

- Owned and operated
- Location and geographic proximity
- Common licensure/accreditation
- Integral and subordinate part
- Administration and supervision
- Clinical services integration
- Financial integration
- Public awareness

Each of these criteria can be further subdivided. Let us take one of them for consideration. Geographic proximity has several aspects. First, the provider-based clinic should be close to the hospital (i.e., the main provider). How close? The default distance is 35 miles. This number is quite arbitrary.* Even if the clinic is outside the 35-mile limit, other criteria can be used to determine if there is an appropriate overlap between the clinic's patients and the

---

* The 35-mile limit comes directly from Congress and is a distance that is also used by the Medicare program as the distance for establishing Sole Community Hospitals, or SCHs.

hospital's patients. If all else fails, the Medicare program can be lobbied to grant an exception.

Second, there is great concern if the clinic is not on the campus of the hospital. If the geographic proximity of the clinic is that it is on-campus (i.e., within 250 yards of the main buildings), then certain special requirements do not have to be met. For off-campus clinics, the special requirements include:

- Physician supervision*
- Emergency Medical Treatment and Labor Act (EMTALA) policy and procedure
- Signage and identification

When services are provided at an off-campus provider-based clinic, a physician or qualified practitioner† must directly supervise‡ the services. Also, if an individual presents to the off-campus provider-based clinic with a potential emergency medical condition, then the clinic must have a policy and procedure in place to address such an occurrence (generally dial "911").§ Also, an individual coming to a provider-based clinic must realize that he is entering hospital premises. Thus, the signage and names used for the clinic must reflect that it is part of the hospital.

This is a brief discussion of only one of the criteria that must be met for a clinic to be provided-based. The others involve many other conditions. Why would a hospital want to go to all of the time and trouble to establish provider-based clinics?

The simple answer is to gain enhanced payment. Overall, provider-based clinics generate more reimbursement. The reason for this is that two different payment systems come together in a rather complex fashion to generate this potential increase in reimbursement. The two payment systems are:

---

* Physician supervision requirements have been updated by CMS Transmittal 82 issued February 8, 2008 and Transmittal 101 issued January 16, 2009. These are updates to CMS Publication 100-02, Medicare Benefit Policy Manual.

† Generally this includes Nurse Practitioners (NPs), Physician Assistants (PAs), or Clinical Nurse Specialists (CNSs).

‡ Physician or qualified practitioner must be in the suite of offices and immediately available.

§ Because the provider-based clinic is hospital property, the EMTALA requirements apply; that is, the emergency department at the hospital should be contacted to send emergency personnel. However, if the clinic is off-campus, this may not be feasible.

1. RBRVS for physician payment
2. APCs for hospital outpatient payment

One is a complex fee schedule and the other is a complex PPS.

Recall from our discussion in Chapter 2 concerning RBRVS that for each CPT/HCPCS code three different RVUs are provided:

1. Work component
2. Practice expense component
3. Medical malpractice component

Additionally, the practice expense RVU is further subdivided into *facility* and *non-facility* RVUs. If a physician is performing services at a facility (i.e., in a provider-based setting), then the physician's overhead or practice expense has been significantly reduced. The provider, generally a hospital, will file a technical component claim using the UB-04 format and be paid for the facility costs.[*]

When you study the individual RVUs you will notice that there is often a difference between the facility and non-facility RVUs. The facility RVU is less than (or sometimes equal to) the non-facility RVU. This difference in RVUs and the associated payment is called the site-of-service (SOS) differential. The physician receives a reduced professional payment if the services are provided in a facility setting.

This SOS differential applies to physicians who provide services in a facility setting. So where do the provider-based clinics come into the picture? Provider-based clinics are generally hospital-based clinics and often the physicians are employed by the hospital. Thus the hospital is essentially filing both a 1500 claim form for professional services and also a UB-04 for technical services. Do you think that the combined payments will exceed what the physician would receive in a freestanding clinic? (Another way to ask this, "Is the facility payment greater than the SOS reduction to the physician?")

We will discuss this calculation in a very general form. Actually working with all of the RVUs, geographic adjustment factors, APC payments, and volumes of CPT/HCPCS codes can consume a very large spreadsheet. We will simply look at a single encounter for a Level III evaluation and management (E/M) service described by CPT 99213.

---

[*] Technically, the hospital will be paid for all services/items incident to those of the physician's services. See the Social Security Act §1861(2)(B).

Full physician professional payment at freestanding clinic	$90
SOS reduction	$15
Reduced payment to physician in provider-based clinic	$75
Technical component APC payment to hospital	$50
Total payment to hospital for both professional and technical	$125
Total gain for provider-based clinic versus freestanding clinic	$35

This is a $35 gain for a single code that may be only part of a single encounter. Now the gain varies according to the specific codes involved and everything must be geographically adjusted. However, how much of a gain would be realized if you had 5,000 visits or 20,000 visits? The gain can become significant in larger hospital settings running into the millions of dollars.

Provider-based clinics and the PBR represent a very interesting example of rules and regulations developed to control the potential gain that can be realized through the interface of two complex payment systems under the Medicare program.

CASE STUDY 3.5—Provider-Based Clinic at the Summit Nursing Facility

The Summit Nursing Facility is a large SNF located in Anywhere, USA. This is a freestanding entity. With the size of the patient population, particularly the large number of Medicare beneficiaries, Summit is considering establishing a provider-based clinic inside of the facility, hiring several physicians and a practitioner or two to staff the clinic 7 days a week with 14-hour coverage.

If you were asked to advise Summit in Case Study 3.5, do you think this is feasible? Legal? What kinds of challenges will be faced? How will the technical component payment be made? Will there be a SOS differential for the physicians and practitioners? What kinds of claims filing will need to be made? Is this type of arrangement financially feasible? What is the overall cost-benefit? For organizing healthcare organizations and delivery systems, a major consideration is financial. The basic question is: How are we going to be paid for providing these healthcare services?

Note: The reality of many organizational issues is that healthcare provider organizations tend to make their decisions on the basis of clinical care for their patients. The financial aspects, including billing and payment issues, are secondary or at least not addressed until after the healthcare services are organized or, sometimes, even after the services are being provided.

Integrated Delivery Systems

An integrated delivery system (IDS) is simply a concept that describes a healthcare delivery system that provides different types of healthcare services. As discussed in the section on freestanding hospitals, a range of different types of services is typically provided through a hospital. Inpatient services, outpatient services, radiology, and physical therapy are among the different services. Thus a typical hospital is really a mini-version of an IDS.

If we move beyond a freestanding healthcare provider such as a single hospital or clinic, there are significant groupings or an integration of different types of healthcare providers. One of the objectives of integrating healthcare providers is to have a *seamless delivery system* in which patients can receive a full spectrum of services from a single integrated organization. In some other instances, organizations may specialize in certain types of service and then develop regional or national systems within the given type of service.

For instance, a company may specialize in providing home health services. Through establishing new HHAs and/or acquiring already existing HHAs, a system of HHAs may be developed. Similarly there are hospital systems, skilled nursing systems, and the list can go on. If these systems are focused on a single type of service, then they are not generally classified as IDSs. From a payment system perspective, developing a chain of HHAs or DME stores does not increase the complexity of addressing payment issues as such. Certainly an increase in volume of claims will result, as will the full range of services within the specific healthcare area. However, the need to deal with hundreds of different payment systems and potential payment system interfaces will not be the result.

With true integration, seamless delivery can occur. Patients may present to a hospital-based clinic, be sent on to the hospital for services, then be moved to a SNF for recovery, and eventually be provided home health services. All of these different types of services can come under the single umbrella of the IDS. Let us visit the Apex Medical Center while they consider a proposal from several other hospitals in their region.

CASE STUDY 3.6—Apex Joining to Form an IDS

The Apex Medical Center is already a mini-IDS. There is a full range of hospital services. Apex owns and operates two SNFs and two HHAs. Apex has 15 provider-based clinics, a joint-venture ASC, and several satellite physical/occupational therapy operations. Apex has now been asked about joining with two other hospitals to form an IDS. One of the hospitals is very similar to Apex and is located approximately 150 miles away. The other hospital is much larger and provides highly specialized services. The IDS is to be a loosely knit organization that is intended to provide better delivery of healthcare services and also a mechanism to negotiate with local third-party payers (TPPs) to gain more favorable contracts for payment.

Note that in this case study, the overall organizational structuring is described as being "loosely knit." In other words, the three hospitals are simply banding together to improve delivery of care and possibly leverage for better payment from private TPPs. The official formation of this IDS may simply be as a joint venture or possibly a partnership or limited liability company.

If the organizational structuring is more formal, we may have situations in which there is a parent company, typically a corporation or not-for-profit organization, that does actually own all of the healthcare providers in the IDS. As you might imagine, the business and organization structuring can become quite complex

Of importance for our discussions are the concerns about payment for a wide variety of healthcare services using possibly hundreds of different payment systems. For a tightly integrated IDS, the billing system may be totally centralized with all claims, both 1500 professional and UB-04 technical, and associated payments being processed through a single monolithic system. The good news for such large organizations is that specialized staff can be developed relative to different payment systems. For instance, inpatient Medicare DRG expertise, outpatient Medicare APC expertise, physician RBRVS expertise, private contract expertise, and the like can all be developed through specialized personnel.

Special Organizational Structuring

There are very few limits in structuring healthcare provider organizations. Much of the organizational activity surrounds the rules and regulations with the Medicare program. We will look at one of many examples of what can be considered to be special in some sense. The example we will use is the concept of a hospital-within-a-hospital (HwH).

This particular approach is typically used when a specialty hospital is to be established and the owners of the specialty hospital really do not want to build a whole new physical structure along with the infrastructure that is needed. The basic idea is for the specialty hospital to be located right inside of the host hospital. The host hospital is typically a short-term acute-care hospital although this model can be used with highly variable combinations. Let us visit the Apex Medical Center relative to a proposal that is being made concerning the establishment of a specialty orthopedic hospital within the Apex Medical Center.

CASE STUDY 3.7—Orthopedic Specialty Hospital within a Short-Term Acute-Care Hospital

A group of orthopedic surgeons has approached the Apex Medical Center about establishing a specialty hospital inside Apex itself. Because of shifting population and service patterns, Apex has an entire surgical floor that is now essentially empty. Although some of the space is being used for a variety of administrative purposes, this space can easily be converted to provide orthopedic specialty surgeries. The group of surgeons wants services such as maintenance, housekeeping, laundry, central supplies, pharmacy, and other infrastructure activities to be provided by the host hospital. The new specialty hospital would simply rent the space and all of the services from Apex.

Although this case study is oversimplified, the idea is reasonably straightforward. The immediate question that should arise is whether or not there will be any payment system concerns relative to this arrangement. As you might quickly conclude, the Medicare program does have some concerns, and several complex rules and regulations concerning the relationship between the host hospital and the specialty hospital must be considered.

Summary and Conclusion

Organization of healthcare services and the associated provider organizations ranges from the very simple to the highly complex. We started this discussion with a solo physician practice in which the payment systems used revolve around fee schedule payment. By moving to a freestanding hospital the complexity of the payment systems escalates rapidly. If we move all of the way up the complexity scale, we encounter systems of hospitals and then various types of IDSs. The number and type of payment systems for even modest-sized IDSs become significant, and the complexity of billing and claims filing also become increasingly complex. This discussion will be extended somewhat in Chapter 5 when various types of healthcare providers gain billing privileges, particularly with the Medicare program and the different CMS-855 forms.

Chapter 4

Revenue Cycle versus Reimbursement Cycle

Introduction

Healthcare payment systems typically provide payment for services provided, supplies dispensed, drugs provided, and various combinations of services. Many of these payment systems are generally classified as fee-for-service systems in which payment is made based on the services provided. In Chapter 2 we discussed various types of payment systems, most of which are generally fee-for-service. These types of payment systems involved billing or filing claims for services.

In this chapter we will briefly discuss the reimbursement cycle. The reimbursement cycle is a major subset of the revenue cycle. The revenue cycle takes into account all income or payments being provided to a healthcare provider, regardless of the source. The reimbursement cycle involves those cases in which a bill and associated claim for services, supplies, and other items is generated and payment is received typically from the third-party payer (TPP).

The Reimbursement Cycle

Figure 4.1 shows a generalized chart of the hospital reimbursement cycle. This chart can be modified for other types of healthcare providers. The basic ideas involve the encounter, provision of services, documentation of

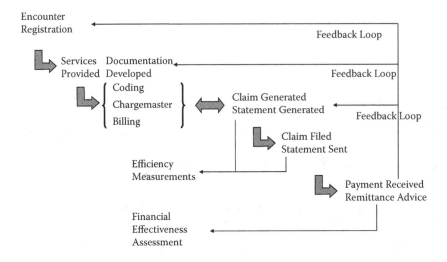

Figure 4.1 Hospital reimbursement cycle.

services, billing for services, filing a claim, and then eventually payment for the claim filed.

Other types of payment systems use different units of service such as per diem or a 60-day period. In a physician's office or clinic setting, there is no chargemaster, but there is still some sort of a charge schedule or physician fee schedule. For nursing homes or Home Health Agencies the coding process is much more dependent on documentation development through extensive assessment forms. However, the general concept of the reimbursement cycle is the same across different healthcare providers and even payment systems as long as a claim is filed and adjudicated, and payment is made.

The revenue cycle is broader. There may be income streams that do not arise because of billing and filing a claim with a TPP. For instance, hospitals typically have physical therapy (PT) and occupational therapy (OT) services. Patients may be sent to the hospital to receive such services and the hospital does bill and file claims with TPPs for payment. The hospital may also contract with Skilled Nursing Facilities (SNFs) to provide PT/OT services to the SNF's residents. For the Medicare program, these PT/OT services provided to the SNF residents are paid through the SNF payment system. In this case the consolidated billing process is in connection with Resource Utilization Groups (RUGs). Thus, the hospital will bill the SNF under the provisions of a contract for PT/OT services. Revenue is thus generated that is not the result of filing a claim with a TPP of some sort.

Optimizing the Reimbursement Cycle

There are two main approaches for optimizing the reimbursement cycle: (1) efficiency, and (2) effectiveness. These two approaches are not necessarily exclusive. The efficiency approach concentrates on performing the different tasks within the system (in this case the cycle) faster and quicker (i.e., with greater efficiency). For instance, financial personnel are very interested in cash flow and the time value of money. Thus, their concern with the reimbursement cycle, or more generally the revenue cycle, is to do anything to get the money in the door more quickly. Thus metrics like days in A/R (account receivable) become important. Questions such as "Can we get the coding done more quickly?" or "Can we get the charges input more timely?" are important. The actual generation of claims is a computer process. The only real way to speed up the claims generation is to get the necessary information into the billing system more quickly.

The effectiveness approach generally concentrates more on quality than on speed or quickness, for instance, developing better, more complete documentation, or identifying services or items that are not being charged (i.e., charge capture). Effectiveness measures tend to require more in-depth work, analysis, and thought. Flowcharting techniques, interviews, and analysis of various flows are all good techniques among many others.

The reimbursement cycle illustrated in Figure 4.1 is generalized. For hospitals, this same chart may need to be refined down to the department or service-area level. If we translate this type of flow into a physician's office, it may become a little simpler. However, you may be involved in a multispecialty clinic that is part of an integrated delivery system so that a detailed reimbursement cycle chart would become quite complicated.

Final Product

For our purposes, the final product is the claim that is generated. Of course the claim must be filed and adjudicated, and payment received. However, for payment system purposes we want to generate a good, clean, complete, and accurate claim. This is much easier said than done.

Whenever we study, analyze, and audit the reimbursement cycle we must take into account multiple factors. For a given TPP, using a specific payment system with specific claims filing requirements, we can trace through the overall reimbursement cycle. In some cases certain types of documentation may be required, in others special coding requirements are the norm, while in yet other cases charges may be delimited. The number of variations that are generated given dozens if not hundreds of TPPs, and then all of the different payment systems involved, make optimizing the reimbursement cycle a major ongoing challenge.

Systems theory tells us that to meet our goal of generating a good, clean, complete, and accurate claim, we must work backwards through the system flow. Only with a good claim will we be properly paid for services provided and items supplied. The way in which a given payment system reimburses for services and items will affect the overall process. For instance, many hospital inpatient payment systems do not pay separately for pharmaceutical items. Thus, for a hospital, capturing charges for drugs is important but there is no direct reimbursement loss. However, many hospital outpatient payment systems do pay for pharmacy items separately so that charges must be captured, and the drugs coded with proper units, and these drugs must appear on the claim according to TPP requirements.

Key Features in the Reimbursement Cycle

A complete discussion of the reimbursement cycle is well beyond the scope of this book. However, there are some very important features and points of consideration within this cycle. We will briefly point these out, keeping in mind that our context is healthcare payment systems.

Note that in Figure 4.1 there are several feedback loops. As services are provided, documentation developed, and claims generated, there may be problems noted at different points within this systematic process. Feedback should always be provided back to the point in the overall system where problems are occurring. In some cases it seems to be easier to just fix claim downstream or at the very end of the process, but this is certainly not the best practice.

There are challenges at every step within this overall process. At the very beginning is the patient registration. In some cases this is a very innocuous point in the process. A patient going to a physician's office simply checks in at the registration desk. Of course, it would be very nice if we could verify primary and secondary insurance coverage, the reason for the visit, and any unusual factors surrounding the visit. Another example is a patient presenting to a hospital outpatient surgery department. In addition to all of the usual forms that must be signed, the given service may require a pre-authorization from the insurance company or what we have generically called a TPP.

For payment purposes, if a service provided or item supplied is not documented, then it never happened. Thus documentation becomes important both clinically and for payment purposes. For the reimbursement cycle illustrated in Figure 4.1, there are two types of documentation of interest:

1. Clinical documentation
2. Financial documentation

Clinical documentation in terms of the medical records, or what is sometimes referred to as the patient's record, is well known. For payment purposes the services provided and items supplied must be documented, including medical necessity justification. There is also financial information that is developed as services are provided. In the hospital setting this may encompass a charge sheet, order entry, charge entry, and associated mechanism for charging for services. Other types of healthcare providers have similar mechanisms for developing charges and then the associated codes that must be used on claim forms. As discussed in Chapter 2, some payment systems can be heavily driven by specific types of documentation, including the use of extensive forms. With payment systems of this type, the development of the charge or related financial information may be rather minimal.

All of the steps within the reimbursement cycle are under the control of the healthcare provider, except for the claim adjudication process through which the TPP determines the amount to be paid. Although a healthcare provider cannot control the adjudication process as such, the exact way in which claims are processed and adjudicated can be known. It is this knowledge that drives the overall development of charges, the claim, documentation, prior approval, and the like. The more a healthcare provider knows about the adjudication process, the more likely claims will be properly developed, resulting in quick adjudication and payment.

Regardless of the type of healthcare provider, all healthcare providers are businesses. Businesses must make money simply to stay in business. The final step and overall goal of the reimbursement cycle is to be paid for healthcare services of all types. Note that there is an additional note that addresses the overall financial effectiveness. Although we tend to monitor overall payments by different TPPs and then even with specific payment systems for a given TPP, overall financial profitability must occur or the business will fail.

Although healthcare providers must be viable businesses, integrated delivery systems have the luxury of being able to operate certain business functions at a loss to sustain some other service lines. For instance a large hospital may have several provider-based clinics that run at a loss, but the clinics funnel patients into the hospital for inpatient and outpatient services.

Special Software Interfaces

In larger healthcare provider settings, such as hospitals and integrated delivery systems, the overall billing and claims generation process may involve other computer systems that interface to the main billing system. We can generally categorize these as *front-end* and *back-end systems.*

In a hospital setting certain departments may have their own computer systems. For instance, the surgery department may have a surgery information system. Quite often pharmacies also have their own systems. Although these front-end systems may be designed for clinical purposes, they often also provide information that is passed over to the main hospital billing system. If the interfaces between these special front-end systems and the main billing system are not properly synchronized, claims may not be properly generated and the reimbursement cycle breaks down to some extent.

Back-end systems are generally devoted to claims scrubbing and editing. For instance, a back-end system may contain special editing software to identify claims that fail any special edits for a given TPP. The Medicare program has the National Correct Coding Initiative (NCCI) edits. Other TPPs may also have various edits that must be checked. Note that these back-end systems may do more than just edit and identify questionable claims; these systems may have programmed logic that actually changes the claim that is generated from the main billing system.

Note: One of the challenges with both front-end and back-end computer systems that are separate from the main billing system is whether or not these systems can properly communicate. There is a standard interface specification, Health Level 7 (HL-7), which addresses this communication interface issue. This standard falls under the Health Insurance Portability and Accountability Act (HIPAA) Administrative Simplification legislation.

For each and every healthcare provider the reimbursement cycle is a complex process that must be flexible enough to accommodate varying demands from TPPs and a host of different payment systems. The general process is fairly simple; that is, encounter patients, provide services, document, bill, file a claim, and be paid. However, when you start factoring into this process the many different payment systems, coding systems, documentation systems, special requirements, and the like, this process becomes quite complex.

Payment System Interfaces

A major challenge for healthcare providers of all types, and particularly those that are involved in integrated delivery systems, is that payment systems are often designed to address a particular type of service and/or a particular type of healthcare provider. There can be different types of healthcare providers associated with providing the same service. This involves possibly providing the same type of service in different settings and potentially with different types of providers, which, in turn, involves different payment systems.

We can also look at this from the perspective of a given service being paid by two, or sometimes three, different TPPs. Consider a primary payer and a secondary payer. The primary and secondary payers may have vastly different payment systems in use. The Medicare program has even established a major initiative, the Medicare Secondary Payer (MSP) program. Medicare pays out literally millions of dollars a year for services that are actually the responsibility of some other payer. Also, it is likely that the other payer uses a different payment system.

CASE STUDY 4.1—Elderly Patient Accidental Fall

Sarah was visiting her son's home when she took a tumble down the landing. Her son and daughter-in-law took her to the Apex Medical Center's emergency department (ED). Luckily it was only a sprain, a stabilizing wrap was applied, and pain medication was administered.

In Case Study 4.1, is the Medicare program primary? No, the accident occurred at her son's home. Thus, the medical payments and liability insurance are primary and Medicare is secondary. The question then becomes "Will this critical information be obtained so that the correct insurer and associated payment system will be used?"

There may also be differences in claims filing requirements between the primary and secondary payers and their associated payment systems.

CASE STUDY 4.2—Nonselective Renal Angiography after Heart Catheterization

The coding and billing staff at the Apex Medical Center has carefully altered the billing system so that Medicare claims including a nonselective renal angiography after a heart catheterization* are correctly coded with a Healthcare Common Procedure Coding System (HCPCS) code, namely G0275. However, for other TPPs, this service is coded using the normal Current Procedural Terminology (CPT) sequence of codes.

The Medicare Recovery Audit Contractors (RACs) target many of their recoupment efforts in areas in which there is a payment system interface. A favorite area of investigation is short-stay inpatient admissions that could or should have been outpatient observation services.

CASE STUDY 4.3—Inpatient Admission after Outpatient Surgery

In the morning an elderly patient has presented for cataract surgery. Because of the nervousness of the patient, general anesthesia is provided. The surgery proceeds normally. However, in recovery the patient experiences some cardiac arrhythmias and the physician decides to admit the patient to the hospital. Later that afternoon, the patient has fully recovered and the physician discharges the patient home.

In Chapter 3 we discussed one of the most complex interfaces involving provider-based clinics. This is an example of the interface between the Medicare hospital outpatient prospective payment system, Ambulatory

---

* This type of angiography may be referred to as a "drive-by shooting" because as the catheter is withdrawn down the aorta, it is simply stopped at the renal level and an angiography is performed.

Payment Classifications (APCs), and the physician payment system, the Medicare Physician Fee Schedule (MPFS), which is based on the Resource-Based Relative Value System (RBRVS). Similarly, in Chapter 1 we discussed different types of healthcare providers. As an individual moves from one type of provider to another, the payment systems may also change and will necessarily need to interface in some way. For instance, if a Medicare patient has been in a short-term acute-care hospital and then moves to a SNF, there is a 3-day inpatient stay that is required for Medicare to cover the SNF services.

Payment system interfaces abound. Regardless of the specific provider setting in which you are working, look for different challenges involving more than one payer or more than one payment system. In the following we will look at some simple examples as case studies of these payment system interfaces. Most of these case studies come from the many different payment systems developed and utilized by the Medicare program.

CASE STUDY 4.4—Inpatient-Only Surgery Provided as an Outpatient

- An elderly patient is scheduled to have outpatient surgery today. The surgery proceeds as scheduled but the surgeon runs into some complications and a more extensive surgery is required. The surgery is successfully completed, the patient is taken to recovery, then extended recovery, and stays overnight in observation. The patient is discharged home in the afternoon. Utilization review personnel review the case several days later only to discover that the surgery performed is on the Medicare inpatient-only list.

Case Study 4.4 is not unusual. The propriety of performing any given surgery in a given setting, in this case as an outpatient, is really a medical judgment made by the surgeon. However, the Medicare program has decided that certain surgeries will be paid only if the surgery is performed on an inpatient basis. If for some untoward reason the surgery is performed on an outpatient basis, then Medicare will not pay for the surgery and the Medicare beneficiary becomes liable to pay for the surgery.

This is an example of the inpatient payment system, Diagnosis-Related Groups (DRGs), interfacing to the outpatient payment system, APCs. Given the potential reaction of a Medicare beneficiary receiving a bill for the surgery, hospitals typically write-off these types of situations. Luckily there is an exception to this policy if a patient is rushed to the ED and then taken to surgery, an inpatient-only surgery is performed, and the patient expires. In cases like this, the individual may never be officially admitted as an inpatient. The APC payment system has a special mechanism to pay for these types of cases using a special modifier.*

CASE STUDY 4.5—Durable Medical Equipment to Medicare Hospital Inpatients

Sam, a retired farmer, has been in the hospital recovering from an accident. The day before he is to go home, a durable medical equipment (DME) provider comes to the hospital, fits a brace, and instructs Sam and his wife on the use of the brace. The DME supplier bills the hospital for the device, the time for fitting and training, mileage to and from the hospital, and other incidental expenses.

Sam's hospital stay is paid through the inpatient prospective payment system DRGs. This payment system is highly inclusive and includes all supplies, devices, drugs, and services that are provided during the inpatient stay. However, DME is generally paid through an extensive fee schedule and must be billed by a DME supplier who enrolls with Medicare by filing a CMS-855-S form. With the general facts in Case Study 4.5, DME provided a day or two before the patient is discharged home is not part of the DRG payment and is to be billed by the DME supplier.

Here is another case study involving DME.

CASE STUDY 4.6—Crutches, Canes, and Walkers for ED Patients

The Apex Medical Center is not a DME supplier. However, there are occasions in which Medicare beneficiaries present to the ED after hours with conditions that require crutches, canes, and/or

---

* The modifier is the HCPCS "-CA" modifier that has the description: "Procedure payable only in the inpatient setting when performed emergently on an outpatient who expires prior to admission."

walkers. In cases like this, Apex simply loans the necessary device to the patient. However, these crutches, canes, and walkers are rarely returned to the hospital.

The basic circumstances of this case study arise at almost every hospital that has an ED. Although there are many variations on the solution provided in Case Study 4.6, most of these solutions are really not appropriate. Crutches, canes, and walkers are DME and should be billed by a DME supplier. These items are not part of the payment that hospitals receive for outpatient ED services through APCs. This case study also illustrates that compliance issues can be invoked when involved with payment system interfaces. Giving away DME could be considered as providing an inducement to gain more business. At a purely business level, why would a business give away relatively expensive items such as crutches, canes, and walkers?

CASE STUDY 4.7—Hyperbaric Oxygen to SNF Residents

The community physicians are excited that the Apex Medical Center has established a hyperbaric oxygen (HBO) facility. The physicians are anxious to start prescribing HBO to several SNF residents relative to wound care.

Case Study 4.7 seems to be a situation in which appropriate services can be provided to SNF residents. However, the excitement around a HBO program for SNF patients may be short lived. HBO services are considered to be part of the SNF consolidated payment. The hospital cannot bill the Medicare program for these HBO services. The SNF must pay the hospital for these services. This again illustrates what happens when payment systems must be interfaced with each other.

CASE STUDY 4.8—Physical Therapist Called to ED

The ED at the Apex Medical Center is quite busy. There is a Medicare patient that has presented with a badly sprained shoulder. A special splint needs to be fabricated and applied. The ED physicians do not have time to do this, so a physical therapist is called who provides the necessary services.

The basic facts in Case Study 4.8 appear to be quite straightforward; however, there are really two different payment systems involved. Physical therapy services are typically paid through the MPFS. The billing will be on the UB-04 claim form and a special HCPCS modifier, the "-GP," "services delivered under an outpatient physical therapy plan of care" must be used. However, in this particular case there is no physical therapy plan of care; these services are being provided in the ED on an outpatient basis. Thus payment should be made by the hospital outpatient payment system, namely APCs. Thus, the claim will need to be filed without the "-GP" modifier.

CASE STUDY 4.9—DRG Pre-Admission Window

The Apex Medical Center owns and operates a freestanding clinic about 20 miles from the hospital. An elderly patient presented to the clinic on Tuesday complaining of cough, congestion, and fever. A workup was performed, including radiology and laboratory tests. An antibiotic was prescribed. On Thursday evening the patient presents through the ED with much worse symptoms and is diagnosed with pneumonia. The patient is admitted and stays in the hospital for 4 days.

In Case Study 4.9, the diagnostic services provided at the clinic as well as any therapeutic services related to the pneumonia will have to be billed through the hospital. The DRG pre-admission window requires that certain services, if provided within three dates-of-service prior to an admission, must be bundled into the inpatient billing. This is a good example of a fairly well-defined interface between inpatient and outpatient services and the associated billing and payment.

Summary and Conclusion

We have briefly discussed the reimbursement cycle and then looked at an associated topic—payment system interfaces. The reimbursement cycle is a large subset of the slightly broader revenue cycle. Reimbursement for our purposes implies that a claim has been filed and adjudicated, and then payment provided. Given the spectrum of healthcare providers and then all of the many payment systems that are used to pay for healthcare services, the reimbursement cycle is really a general systematic approach that must be modified to meet the needs of a given type of healthcare provider and then also meet the needs of the payment systems used to reimburse the given healthcare provider.

If for each healthcare provider the reimbursement cycle were discrete (i.e., a healthcare provider simply provided services, filed a claim, and was paid) life would be reasonably straightforward. Healthcare providers interact in providing services and thus there can be a great deal of interaction of the payment systems. Even if there is an integrated delivery system with seamless delivery, the interaction of the payment systems still occurs. Several simple case studies have been provided to illustrate some of these payment system interfaces. In practice, these payment system interfaces abound. Even if we focus on the Medicare payment systems, these systems are not necessarily designed to smoothly interface. Thus healthcare providers must constantly study the payment systems and watch for interface problems. These interfaces provide significant opportunities for auditors to identify possible overpayments. Such is the case with Medicare's RAC program.

Chapter 5

Chapter 5

Claims Generation and Adjudication

Introduction

Chapter 4 discussed the difference between the *revenue cycle* and the *reimbursement cycle*. For many, if not most, healthcare payment systems, some sort of claim or bill must be submitted for payment. As discussed in Chapter 2, the billing and associated payment process should be between the patient and the healthcare provider. However, most often there are third-party payers (TPPs) of various types that come into this payment process. Given the complexity of the payment systems themselves, there is an added complexity in billing and claim filing for healthcare services. Even before claims can be filed, processed, and then paid, the given healthcare provider may need to be qualified by the payer so that such claims can even be accepted and processed for payment using the given payment system.

Because of the wide array of circumstances, healthcare providers filing claims find themselves addressing different levels of formality relative to being qualified to file claims. In addition to generally discussing the billing, claims filing, and adjudication processes, we will address three levels of formality for qualifying to be able to file claims and be reimbursed. This discussion will then be correlated to the Health Insurance Portability and Accountability Act (HIPAA) Transaction Standard/Standard Code Set (TSC) rule in Chapter 6.

Keep in mind that the general requirements for a TPP to pay for services are:

- The patient must be covered.
- The services rendered and items dispensed must be covered.
- The services are ordered and provided by a qualified medical persons.
- The services are medically necessary.
- The services must be appropriately documented.
- A correct claim is filed on a timely basis.

If all of these general requirements are met, a claim can be generated and processed with payment made through the given payment system being used. As we will see in Chapter 6, this whole process should be electronic and occur within a matter of minutes. The reality for claims adjudication is that it may take days, weeks, or sometimes months.

Three Levels of Formality for Claim Filing

Most healthcare providers file claims under three different levels of formality. Although there is no standard terminology, we will use:

1. Statutory
2. Contractual
3. General

Our greatest concentration throughout this book is the Medicare program, which is statutorily established. Through a hierarchical process the laws passed by Congress eventually result in rules and regulations issued by CMS (Centers for Medicare & Medicaid Services) that direct healthcare providers on how, when, and in what form to file claims. The Medicare program payment systems and payment processes are both the most complicated and at the same time the most public. Note also that the various Medicare, Medicaid, and other governmental programs change, sometimes rapidly, over time. Because the Medicare program is statutorily established, failure to faithfully follow the various rules and regulations when filing claims can result in both civil and criminal penalties.

The contractual level occurs when a healthcare provider enters into a contract with a given TPP. Such contracts can be voluminous, although in many cases the actual contract is relatively brief. For brief contracts there are usually references to other guidance (possibly companion) manuals that direct the healthcare provider on when, where, and how to file claims. For these contractual situations, the details of the payment system and sometimes the details on exactly how to file claims can be ambiguous. Also, change is ever present so that healthcare providers must constantly study and revise the way in which claims are filed. From a compliance perspective, these contracts establish obligations on both parties. If there are disagreements, then civil proceedings are the norm.

The third level involves situations in which a healthcare provider is filing a claim, on behalf of a patient, to a payer that may be completely unknown to the healthcare provider. There are no contractual arrangements; there are no coding, billing, and claims filing guidelines. Basically, the healthcare provider is filing the claim and then hoping that the claim will be properly adjudicated and payment made. Actually, the full claim should be paid; however, often the payer may choose to pay the claim on the basis of some payment system developed by the payer.

For this third level, what rules or guidelines should the healthcare provider follow? The answer is that the guidelines to follow come from the HIPAA TSC rule. We will discuss this in Chapter 6. Briefly, the HIPAA TSC rule gives healthcare providers standard claim formats, standard code sets, and standard electronic processes for filing claims and receiving payment.

Note: As we will discuss in Chapter 6, the HIPAA TSC should allow all healthcare providers, for a given service, to file the same claim in a standard format to all payers. Thus our discussion about statutory and contractual requirements for coding, billing, and filing claims should not even be an issue. Today's reality is that payers make demands relative to claim development to accommodate the payers' adjudication of the claims for their particular payment system.

Medicare Conditions for Payment

The Medicare program has a formal, complex process for gaining billing privileges. The Conditions for Payment (CfP) under the Medicare program can be found in the *Code of Federal Regulations* (CFR) at 42 CFR §424. In this CFR section, general rules and regulations relating to claims filing and billing for Medicare beneficiaries are discussed at some length. If you are involved with any healthcare provider that files claims with the Medicare program, then you should read this section of the CFR.

CASE STUDY 5.1—Delayed Charges

Patient financial services at the Apex Medical Center have just been contacted by one of the newer service areas. It appears that there are several hundred cases in which charges were not completely posted into the billing system. In a few cases, no charges at all were posted. The cases involve Medicare, Medicaid, and several other private TPPs.

One of the general requirements for claims filing is that the claim must be filed in a timely manner. What the word *timely* means can vary. The CFR section for the CfP provides for a rather complicated algorithm to determine how far back claims can be filed and/or refiled with changes. In general, private TPPs want claims filed fairly quickly (i.e., within a few months of the services being provided). Additionally, some states have laws that delimit the time period during which claims can be filed and payment made. For instance, a state law may require that any such transactions be completed within a 1-year period.

When you read the CfP section of the CFR, you will quickly understand that the Medicare program is greatly concerned about the process of making payments to healthcare providers. Basically, the Medicare program is concerned about fraudulent claims and then the resulting incorrect payment. Given the wide range of healthcare provides, it is not unusual for a healthcare provider to reassign its payments to a billing company or a parent organization. This process of reassignment, at least for the Medicare program, must be taken quite seriously and fastidiously kept up to date. We will encounter the CMS-855-R ("R" for reassignment) form in the next section. Let us consider a case study involving a single practitioner.

CASE STUDY 5.2—Nurse Practitioner Reassignment

A nurse practitioner (NP) is employed by the Apex Medical Center. In the mornings the NP provides pre-surgery history and physical (H&P) examinations. In the afternoons, the NP sees patients at a freestanding clinic owned and operated by the Apex Medical Center. Several evenings each week, the NP provides emergency room (ER) coverage for a small hospital approximately 40 miles away. The NP has an NPI number and professional billing is performed. In each case the Medicare payments are reassigned. For the pre-surgery H&Ps, the reassignment is to the Apex Medical Center. For the clinic work, the reassignment is to the clinic itself. For the ER work, the reassignment is to the smaller hospital.

Note also that in situations like those described in Case Study 5.2, arrangements can and do change with some frequency. For instance, the NP in our case study might be moved to a provider-based clinic for the afternoon services or a new mobile clinic might be established. Each time there is a change, the CMS-855-R must be updated and refiled with the appropriate Medicare Administrative Contractor (MAC).

Gaining Medicare Billing Privileges

The process of obtaining and maintaining billing privileges with the Medicare program involves completing, filing, and obtaining approval through the CMS-855 form. Actually, there are five different forms.

1. CMS-855-A, Part A: Hospitals
2. CMS855-B, Part B: Clinics
3. CMS-855-I: Individuals
4. CMS-855-R: Reassignment
5. CMS-855-S: Durable Medical Equipment (DME) Prosthetics, Orthotics, Supplies (DMEPOS) suppliers

With the exception of the 855-R, which is relatively short, the other forms are long and involved, and require additional information as attachments. Of utmost importance is that these forms must be updated whenever there is a change. As we will see in some simple case studies, for a healthcare provider of any size and diversity, there will be dozens if not hundreds of CMS-855 forms to keep up to date. Given that these forms must be manually updated* and that the associated attachments and additional information

---

* At some point in the future, it may be possible that these forms can be updated electronically. However, because these are legal documents, appropriate signatures must be obtained.

must also be updated, someone in the healthcare provider organization will need to devote some real time and effort to this process.

What does the Medicare program want to know about a healthcare provider that will file claims and be reimbursed? Basically, here are the key elements:

- Who are you?
- Who owns you?
- Who has financial control over you?
- Who has management control over you?

These questions and the associated answers are quite reasonable, at least conceptually. However, when you start getting into detail, situations can become a little sticky. Consider the following case study for the Apex Medical Center.

CASE STUDY 5.3—Apex Medical Center Board

The Apex Medical Center is a not-for-profit corporation with a board of trustees. Board members are appointed for up to two 3-year terms. Some concern has been raised because the board members are asked to divulge their personal Social Security numbers when they join the board. This is a requirement in filing and updating the CMS-855-A.

Other information that is requested includes items such as physical addresses where services are provided, pay-to address, financial identification numbers (FINs), tax identification numbers (TINs), billing companies, and any compliance issues that have occurred in the past. Because these are legal documents, great care should be taken to obtain the correct, complete information and to be certain that everything is current.

Along with the CMS-855 forms, an auditing program is in place by which CMS can verify that an entity that has billing privileges with the Medicare program does indeed exist and is truly who and what it says it is. The reason for much of this concern is that unscrupulous individuals and organizations have perpetrated significant fraud on the Medicare program.

The number of CMS-855 forms can become voluminous quite quickly. Let us visit the Apex Medical Center as a small, integrated delivery system.

CASE STUDY 5.4—Small, Integrated Delivery System

The Apex Medical Center is the main hospital in a nine-county area. In addition to the main hospital, there are two Skilled Nursing Facilities (SNFs), a Home Health Agency (HHA), a DME supplier, twelve provider-based clinics employing a total of 87 physicians and practitioners, a joint venture Ambulatory Surgical Center (ASC), an off-campus dialysis center, and an off-campus diagnostic testing facility.

The immediate question is how many CMS-855 forms are required for Apex as a small, integrated delivery system (IDS)? Without more explicit information (e.g., How are the clinics organized? Are the physicians all in a group practice?), the exact number of CMS-855 forms is difficult to determine. There will certainly be one for the hospital, probably two for the SNFs, another for the HHA, another as a DME supplier, one for the ASC, one or more for the clinics, and probably two each for each physician and practitioner. Each physician and practitioner, with the exception of any Physician Assistants (PAs), will need both a CMS-855-I and a CMS-855-R. PAs do not need the 855-R because payment for PAs must be made to the PA's employer. Although there is no information about ambulance services and other types of providers that might be under the IDS umbrella, addressing the CM-855 situation for just the Medicare program is a significant task.

Note: In Chapter 6 we will discuss the associated concept of the National Provider Identifiers (NPIs). Just at the Medicare enrollment forms must be updated to reflect any changes, the information provided to the NPI enumerator must also be kept up to date. We also discussed the Provider-Based Rule (PBR) in Chapter 3 and this rule also has reporting requirements to keep information up to date.

Gaining Billing Privileges with Private TPPs

Obtaining billing privileges with insurance companies and other private TPPs is generally much easier than with the Medicare or Medicaid programs. In some instances healthcare providers must file claims with payers with which the provider has no relationship at all.

If there is a contractual arrangement between the healthcare provider and the TPP, then typically some sort of credentialing or enrollment will be required. The payer needs to know that the healthcare provider is qualified to provide services and then to bill and file claims for services. For instance, a hospital must be duly licensed at the state level. A physician must be licensed and appropriately credentialed. There may be other specific requirements relative to prescribing and/or dispensing pharmaceutical items.

Because significant variability exists in gaining billing privileges, and the requirements and applications involved depend on the specific TPP involved, we will not attempt to categorize all of the possibilities. For our purposes, for a healthcare payment system and TPPs using a healthcare payment system to make payment, there are certain requirements and qualifications that must be met by the healthcare provider. For the Medicare program these are quite extensive; for other private TPPs there can be great variability.

CASE STUDY 5.5—Billing Privileges for Non-Physician Practitioners

The Acme Medical Clinic is owned and operated by a group of physicians. There are also two NPs and a PA that are employed by the clinic. These three Non-Physician Practitioners (NPPs) are fully recognized by the Medicare program and payment processes are well delineated. However, Acme is having great difficulties in obtaining billing privileges for these NPPs from several large insurance companies in the community. It appears that the NPPs can perform services, but the physicians must bill. Given the nature of services provided by the NPPs, the clinic would like these individuals admitted to the insurance company panels of recognized providers.

Case Study 5.5 illustrates one of many potential frustrations. The Medicare program in some respects has blazed a trail in recognizing NPPs and then adjusting the payment systems to provide reimbursement. Private payers may or may not recognize these practitioners for billing purposes.

Preparing and Filing Claims

In Chapter 6 we will discuss the HIPAA TSC rule. In theory this rule provides all healthcare providers the opportunity to use electronic data interchange (EDI) for billing and filing claims. Although achieving the goal of everything being electronic may take many years, at the very least health-care providers can have a standard, uniform way to file claims.

The two most frequently utilized claim forms are:

1. 1500 (for Medicare the CMS-1500)
2. UB-04 (for Medicare the CMS-1450)

The 1500 claim for is for professional billing and the UB-04 claim form is for facility or institutional billing. However, these claim forms can be used in different ways depending upon the context. For example, Critical Access Hospitals (CAHs) can elect Method II payment bill for physician services on the UB-04 instead of on the 1500. In other instances, a given TPP may require the use of the 1500 form to include certain facility charges.

In actuality, we should not even be discussing these two claim forms. Instead we should be discussing the detailed format specifications for the electronic version of these two claims forms, namely the HIPAA 837P (the "P" is for professional) and the HIPAA 837I (the "I" is for institutional).

As you can probably envisage, with the many different payment systems using a multitude of code sets, filing claims can become a very complex process. Add into this mix the fact that Medicare, Medicaid, and many, if not most, of the private payers make special demands, learning all of the nuances of claims filing, even with a limited set of services, is a major undertaking.

Coding and billing personnel for any healthcare provider that routinely files claims fight an almost daily battle to file claims correctly, use the proper codes, and meet special TPP demands, and then hope that proper payment results. For some services, prior approval must be gained from the TPP. Although the exceptions are few, there are some instances for certain health-care providers that revert to the most fundamental payment system (i.e., cash payment) up front even before the services are provided.

CASE STUDY 5.6—Plastic Surgeon Comes to Anywhere, USA

Anywhere, USA, has the good fortune of having a plastic surgeon come to town. A solo practice has been established. The plastic surgeon is very selective with patients. The plastic surgeon has opted out of Medicare, but will see a Medicare patient on a private contract basis. All services are provided in a freestanding ambulatory surgery facility that is part of the plastic surgeon's office. All services must be paid in advance. No claims are filed. Patients can arrange for easy payments and/or loans through the clinic. Of course, credit cards are certainly accepted.

Case Study 5.6 is certainly the exception. Most healthcare providers file claims on behalf of their patients to a multitude of payers using highly disparate payment systems.

Claim Adjudication

We have discussed various types of payment systems and we are in the process of going through what is called the reimbursement cycle. Although there are many things that must be accomplished to initially file a claim, after the claim is filed the healthcare provider is at a point of waiting to see how the claim is adjudicated and what sort of (if any) payment will be made.

Healthcare providers cannot control the claims adjudication process as such. What healthcare providers can do is fully understand the payment mechanism and the way in which the claim should be processed. This is much easier said than done. When the claim is adjudicated and payment made, the payer will generally send along an explanation of how the claim was adjudicated. For some TPPs this may be called a remittance advice or some sort of similar terminology

For healthcare providers filing claims, the remittance advice is crucial. Tracking the information provided through the remittance advices provides a mechanism to more fully understand the payment system being used and the way that claims are adjudicated.

CASE STUDY 5.7—Seeking MAC Guidance on Claim Adjudication

Sylvia, the chargemaster coordinator at the Apex Medical Center, has been working with coding and billing staff to resolve the proper way to file claims to the Medicare program. The various manuals and instructions on claim filing have all been reviewed and they now appear to have a solution. As a check to the propriety of their approach, their MAC is contacted. The exact services, codes, and format of the claim are all provided to the MAC representative. The basic question is, "How will this claim be processed?" Surprisingly, the MAC representative responds, "I do not know what will happen; why don't you submit it and see?"

Of course, a wide variety of actions can result from filing a claim. For instance, the claim may be totally rejected because of some error on the claim that does not conform to a given requirement. For the Medicare program this is called *return to provider*, or RTP. Only partial payment may be made because a modifier is missing or there is some other problem with the claim.

Studying payment systems and the associated claim adjudication processes can become a challenge very quickly. Borrowing from the engineering world, we have the two concepts of white- and black-box edits.

For engineering, if we input data into a system, the system processes the data and we then have a resultant output. If this is a white-box process, then we know exactly how the system processes the data. If we are looking at a black-box process, then all we know are the inputs and the resultant outputs. The way the data are processed is not known.

White-box edits are edits or processes within the claims adjudication systems that are fully visible. With study and research these edits can be identified and anticipated; that is, you can properly develop and file your claim to take these edits into account. A good example of an extensive set of white-box edits is the Medicare program's National Correct Coding Initiative (NCCI).* Currently, there are approximately 200,000 edits or code combinations that are not to be used together. These edits apply to the Current Procedural Terminology (CPT) and Healthcare Common Procedure Coding System (HCPCS) code sets and for claims filed by physicians and hospital outpatient services. If for some unusual reason, a code pair should be used together, then a special modifier (i.e., the "-59" distinct procedure) must be used to separate them and gain full payment.

---

* See http://www.cms.hhs.gov/NationalCorrectCodInitEd.

CASE STUDY 5.8—Combination Physical and Occupational Therapy Services

Sarah, an elderly resident of Anywhere, USA, is recovering from an accident. Today she comes to the hospital and has received physical (PT) and occupational therapy (OT) services. The billing personnel at the Apex Medical Center know that certain PT and OT codes are on the NCCI list, and that the "-59" modifier must be used to separate them and gain payment for both services.

Black-box edits are not visible; they are secret. In other words, although we can see the results of these edits by the way in which claims are adjudicated, there is no explicit guidance on even the existence of these edits. The only way you can learn about them is to file claims and then study the remittance advices that accompany the claim payment or nonpayment. Although your study of the given payment system and experience with past claims may indicate that a claim should be processed in a particular manner, you may be surprised to find that the claim is adjudicated differently without any apparent reason.

Black-box edits can, and often do, arise with almost any claims adjudication system; a small example of this concept is the Medicare program's Medically Unlikely Edits (MUEs).* Currently, some of these edits are public and others are not. However, the results of these edits on claims can certainly be noticed. The basic idea is that if a claim contains some sort of aberration that would not normally (but could) be present, then an edit is invoked and full payment is not made.

Black-box edits are a source of significant consternation on the part of coding and billing personnel. As we will discuss in the next section, tracking and studying claims adjudication information is important to fully understand a given payment system and to be able to gain proper payment.

Payment and Claims Reconciliation

After the claim has been filed and adjudicated, and payment has been issued, there should be a tracking or claims reconciliation process on the

---

* See http://www.cms.hhs.gov/NationalCorrectCodInitEd/08_MUE.asp.

part of the healthcare provider. Although checking for proper adjudication and payment makes a great deal of business sense, because the complexities of healthcare payment systems and the resources required to carefully track payments can be significant, not all healthcare providers fastidiously track claims adjudication.

CASE STUDY 5.9—Claims Adjudication Tracking

Sylvia is attending a 2-day workshop on coding, billing, and claims filing. A variety of different types of healthcare providers is attending. She has the opportunity to sit next to a clinic manager of a freestanding clinic in Anywhere, USA. The discussion turns to the topic of tracking claims adjudication information and associated payment. The clinic manager indicates that every single claim is carefully tracked to make certain that full payment is made. Sylvia is somewhat dismayed because at the Apex Medical Center claims of less than $1,000 are never reviewed; that is, the claim is filed and whatever payment is made (or not) is noted, but the claim is not reviewed further.

Physicians, as a group, have long since learned that the investment in the personnel and computer infrastructure to track each and every claim for proper adjudication and payment is well worthwhile. This process includes learning all of the nuances of the payment system in use, claims filing requirements, and any idiosyncrasies in adjudication.

So what if a claim comes back as rejected or only partially paid? The action steps depend on what kind of problem has been encountered. Is it a coding issue? Is something on the claim incorrect? In other words, did the healthcare provider's coding and billing staff make some sort of error? If the specific error can be identified, the claim can be corrected and refiled.

If the specific error cannot be identified, then further research and even inquiries to the TPP may be in order. For the Medicare program you may have to enter into the world of appealing the claim adjudication. Although we will not go through the steps in this formal process, for certain claims, particularly high-volume or high-dollar claims, the appeals process may be appropriate.

Payment to healthcare providers has become automated as much as possible and electronic remittance is generally the rule. Although EDI is the ultimate goal, this goal will not be fully achieved for many years. Additionally, healthcare providers will receive payment from secondary and even tertiary sources, including cash payment from patients for services, deductible amounts, and/or co-payments.

Summary and Conclusion

A brief overview of the general process of developing claims, filing claims, and then understanding the claims adjudication process has been provided. Many things can happen to a claim as it goes through this process, including encountering various edits, denial, suspension, and modification of payment. Healthcare providers of all types must fully understand the payment system involved, any special claims filing requirements, and the way in which the claims will be adjudicated. A key issue in optimizing this process from the healthcare provider's perspective is to carefully track claims adjudication and to fastidiously review claim remittance advice information.

Healthcare providers have different levels of relationships with the different TPPs. For the governmental programs such as Medicare and Medicaid, the relationship is based on statutory laws, rules, and regulations, all of which are voluminous. For certain private payers, the healthcare provider may have a formal contract with the TPP and will thus receive further guidance for properly developing and filing claims. These requirements may be in the contract itself, or more likely in companion manuals or guidance.

If the healthcare provider is developing and filing a claim to a payer with which there is no relationship, a default or general set of rules and regulations comes into play. These are the rules and regulations that have been formalized through the HIPAA TSC rule, which is discussed in the next chapter.

Chapter 6

HIPAA Administrative Simplification

Introduction

In 1996, Congress passed the Health Insurance Portability and Accountability Act (HIPAA; PL 104-191). HIPAA is a major law that will affect healthcare delivery and healthcare compliance for many years to come. There are several different aspects to the HIPAA legislation, including portability and compliance issues. Narrowing our focus to the issues involving payment systems (e.g., coding, billing, reimbursement, and associated healthcare payment processes) only slightly reduces the scope and complexity of the rules that have been developed for this legislation. Many aspects of HIPAA directly impact payment system issues, whereas other features are more incidental to payment processes for healthcare services.

Note: The rules and regulations as developed by the Center for Medicare and Medicaid Services (CMS) for implementation of the HIPAA legislation are found in the *Code of Federal Regulations* (CFR) at 45 CFR §§160, 162, 163. This is a slightly different location from much of the CFR-related Medicare rules that are located within various sections of 42 CFR. We will start with a very brief discussion of HIPAA privacy that indirectly affects certain aspects of healthcare payment systems. We will then discuss what is called the *administrative simplification* part of the HIPAA legislation. The requirements within the administrative simplification directly affect healthcare payment systems and the overall payment process. The main elements of HIPAA administrative simplification involve the HIPAA Transaction Standard/

Standard Code Set (TSC) rule and the National Provider Identifiers (NPIs) that we encountered in Chapter 5.

HIPAA Privacy

The provisions of the HIPAA Privacy Rule went into effect on April 14, 2003, after significant preparation by hospitals, clinics, pharmacies, clearinghouses, insurance companies, and generally what is referred to as *covered entities*. At the time the HIPAA legislation was being finalized by Congress, the privacy portion of this public law was really added in at the last minute. However, the whole area of privacy is certainly a major issue.

The basic idea under the HIPAA Privacy Rule is really quite simple: health information concerning an individual is to be kept confidential and there are strict limits on disclosure. We usually think of HIPAA privacy in terms of medical information or health information, in other words, the medical record, patient record, clinic record, or whatever term might be used in a particular setting.

Congress provided for an extremely broad definition of *protected health information*. Let us start out with the definition of health information.

> ***Health information*** means any information, whether oral or recorded in any form or medium, that:
>
> 1. Is created or received by a healthcare provider, health plan, public health authority, employer, life insurer, school or university, or healthcare clearinghouse; and
> 2. Relates to the past, present, or future physical or mental health or condition of an individual; the provision of healthcare to an individual; or the past, present, or future payment for the provision of healthcare to an individual. (45 CFR §160.103)

The CFR definitions go on to state that protected health information (PHI) is health information that is:

■ Transmitted by electronic media
■ Maintained in electronic media
■ Transmitted or maintained in any other form or medium

A careful reading of the aggregated definition of PHI certainly indicates that almost anything relating to an individual's health falls under this rule. Although we tend to think about PHI in terms of the medical record or clinical services documentation, this definition goes well beyond the classical medical record and includes a great deal of information that is normally within the sphere of coding, billing, reimbursement, and payment systems. This takes us to yet another key definition, namely the designated record set.

> ***Designated record set*** means:
>
> 1. A group of records maintained by or for a covered entity, that is:
>   a. The medical records and **billing records** about individuals maintained by or for a covered healthcare provider;
>   b. The enrollment, payment, claims adjudication, and case or medical management record systems maintained by or for a health plan; or
>   c. Used, in whole or in part, by or for the covered entity to make decisions about individuals.
> 2. For purposes of this paragraph, the term record means any item, collection, or grouping of information that includes protected health information and is maintained, collected, used, or disseminated by or for a covered entity. (45 CFR §164.501)

Note the use of the phrase *billing records* that has been placed in bold. This clearly indicates that any financial information involving billing or filing claims falls squarely under the definition of PHI. Thus, the HIPAA Privacy Rule does affect the overall reimbursement cycle and payment for healthcare services. Additionally, this means that healthcare providers who file claims with various payers must take all appropriate steps to keep such information confidential and to disclose this information only under certain allowable circumstances.

HIPAA TSC Rule

A major part of the HIPAA administrative simplification is the HIPAA TSC rule or the Transaction Standard/Standard Code Set rule. This most directly impacts payment systems through coding, billing, and reimbursement for all types of healthcare providers. Although the overall intent is to standardize and foster electronic data interchange (EDI), there are many different facets to this process. Providers and payers alike are to follow the rules, including clearinghouses and other organizations that process and/or otherwise assist in the transmission and processing of claims.

The basic concept of the HIPAA TSC is fairly simple. There should be standard code sets used in standard formats for electronic submission and processing. In theory, a healthcare provider should be able to provide a service and/or supply items, prepare a claim with the standard code sets in a standard format, and file the standard claim to any third-party payer (TPP). By standardizing this whole process, claims can be processed very quickly, there can be secondary claims crossover that occurs automatically, and payments can be made very quickly.

The HIPAA TSC was fully implemented on October 16, 2003, after a de facto extension of one year. The governmental entity charged with enforcing the HIPAA TSC is CMS. For CMS this means that there is a potential conflict of interest because CMS is administratively in charge of enforcing the various aspects of the HIPAA TSC, and CMS is also administratively in charge of the Medicare program that is a major TPP subject to the provisions of the HIPAA TSC.

Standard Code Sets

There are literally hundreds of standard code sets. In Chapter 2 we briefly mentioned several of the more common and more extensive code sets. These code sets are generally used on either the 1500 claim form (CMS-1500 for the Medicare program) or the UB-04 claim form (CMS-1450 for the Medicare program). A complete study of either of these claim forms and all of the codes on these claims forms can fill several large volumes.

For any standard code set, the key issues are:

■ The code set itself
■ The standard code set maintainer
■ The official guidance for use of the code set

Some of the healthcare payment code sets change frequently, whereas others are fairly stable. Also, some code sets are comprised of hundreds or even thousands of codes whereas others may have less than a hundred entries. Furthermore, some code sets have structured logic to the way in which they have been developed and are organized. Still other code sets are developed on an ad hoc basis and the codes are added or modified as needs arise.

The standard code set maintainer is the all-important entity for any given code set. The code set maintainer is the organization that promulgates, modifies, and adds to the code set. The code set maintainer is also supposed to be the official source for guidance on how the codes are or are not to be used. However, TPPs, with Medicare at the forefront, often impose special use rules on certain codes, code combinations, modifiers, or other aspects of the various code sets. We will briefly review a sampling of code sets.

Current Procedural Terminology—CPT

The American Medical Association (AMA) developed CPT, which is in version 4. The AMA is the standard code set maintainer. Thus new codes, changed codes, deleted codes, and new or changed modifiers all originate from the AMA. Also, the AMA is the official source of guidelines on how to use or not use the CPT codes. However, there are some concerns about guidance because CPT codes are used with several different payment systems.

The format of the CPT codes is generally five digits. These codes are copyrighted.* There are some newer CPT codes that use a five-alphanumeric format with the fifth position being a letter. This is a procedure coding system that has been developed for the use of physicians, practitioners, and certain non-physician providers (e.g., physical therapists). There are thousands of codes and numerous modifiers.

The primary use of CPT is with physicians filing claims under various fee schedule systems. These claims are generally filed on the 1500 claim form. The Medicare program is now also using CPT for outpatient services under the Ambulatory Payment Classification (APC) payment system, which uses the UB-04 claim form. This dual use of CPT codes for physician professional services and hospital technical services does raise issues in interpretation. When professional services are coded under CPT, the process is identifying what services the physician provided. When CPT codes are used for hospitals, the technical component of coding the process is identifying resources that were utilized (e.g., nursing utilization, room, supplies, etc.).

Operationally, healthcare providers must carefully study the coding guidelines that are found in the CPT manual itself and the specific coding guid-

---

* This copyright raises some interesting questions. Where else do you use five-digit numbers?

ance from the many different TPPs, including various edits, special use of modifiers, and special reporting requirements.

The AMA is quite fastidious about updating CPT only once a year, with implementation on January 1 each year. The AMA uses an extensive set of committees to annually study and revise CPT. Although the number of changes can vary from year to year, there are typically hundreds of changes each year. The general organization of the CPT manual is by anatomical site. However, the most frequently used codes, the evaluation and management (E/M) codes, are listed at the beginning of the manual.

Here are a few examples of CPT codes, along with a couple of modifiers:

- 99282—Emergency department visit
- 11600—Excision, malignant lesion including margins, trunk, arms, or legs; excised diameter 0.5 cm or less
- 21800—Closed treatments of rib fracture, uncomplicated, each
- 36430—Transfusion, blood or blood products
- 66984—Extracapsular cataract removal with insertion of intraocular lens
- 71020—Radiologic examination, chest, two views, frontal and lateral
- "-59"—Distinct procedural service
- "-73"—Discontinued outpatient procedure prior to anesthesia administration

Healthcare Common Procedure Coding System—HCPCS

The Health Care Financing Administration (HCFA), which is now CMS, developed the HCPCS code set. Many years ago the original impetus for developing this code set lay with the use of CPT 99070, which is a generic code for supplies. The Medicare program wanted much finer reporting for supplies, and thus this code set was developed to identify specific supplies and has now grown to consume a fairly large manual. Although the word *procedure* occurs in the title of this code set, much of what is in HCPCS involves supplies, drugs, durable medical equipment (DME), and the like. There are some procedure codes. CMS is the official standard code set maintainer, although these codes can also be used for non-Medicare purposes.

The data format is five alphanumeric with the first position being a letter. The letter gives a general indication of the type of items that are included. Modifiers are generally two alphabet characters, although there are some modifiers that include a numeric digit. Here are the general categories sorted by first letter:

A-Codes—General supplies
B-Codes—PEN (Parenteral/Enteral Nutrition) therapy
C-Codes—Special device/supply codes for APCs
D-Codes—Dental codes
E-Codes—DME
G-Codes—Temporary
H-Codes—Alcohol and drug abuse treatment
J-Codes—Drugs
K-Codes—(Temporary)—DME
L-Codes—Orthotic procedures/devices
M-Codes—Medical services
P-Codes—Pathology and laboratory services
Q-Codes—Temporary
R-Codes—Diagnostic radiology
S-Codes—Non-Medicare
T-Codes—For Medicaid use
V-Codes—Vision services/hearing services/speech language pathology
   services

There are also several hundred HCPCS modifiers, some of which can also be used on CPT codes. You may find CPT referred to as "HCPCS Level I'" and then the regular HCPCS code set as "HCPCS Level II" or the national codes. There used to be a Level III HCPCS code set, the local codes, but this code set is no longer in use.

There is a significant update to the HCPCS codes on January 1 of each year, and there are also quarterly updates issued by CMS. These codes are all in the public domain. The biggest challenge in using the HCPCS codes is to determine which kinds of services, and thus which payment systems, use the given codes. For instance, HCPCS L0210 is for a thoracic rib belt. Can hospitals code and bill for this on the UB-04? Or is this DME that must be billed on the 1500 to a DME Regional Carrier? What about a rib belt through a physician's office? What about a Home Health Agency? Or a Skilled Nursing Facility? Obtaining clear, concise answers to these types of questions in using or not using HCPCS codes can be a challenge.

Here are some additional simple examples of HCPCS codes:

- A6457—Tubular dressing with or without elastic, any width, per linear yard
- B4034—Enteral feeding supply kit; syringe-fed, per day
- D5120—Complete denture, mandibular
- E0148—Walker, heavy-duty, without wheels, rigid or folding, any type, each
- G0379—Direct admission of patient for hospital observation care
- J0135—Injection, adalimumab, 20 mg
- Q5001—Hospice care provided in patient's home/residence
- V2200—Sphere, bifocal, plano to plus or minus 4.00d, per lens

Here are two of several hundred modifiers:

- "-QW" – CLIA waived test
- "-F1" – Left hand, second digit

International Classification of Diseases—ICD-9-CM

ICD-9-CM encompasses both a diagnosis coding system (Volumes 1 and 2) along with a procedure coding system (Volume 3). Most of the world has converted to ICD-10 while the United States lags behind. The data format for the ICD-9 is three to five digits. When these codes are represented for human reading, a decimal point is often used. However, inside a computer system the format is five digits, which is the same as CPT.

The World Health Organization develops ICD-9, or ICD-10 for that matter. In the United States, the American Hospital Association is the standard code set maintainer. Interesting enough, with the HIPAA TSC rule, ICD-9 coding is mandated for inpatient coding on the UB-04.

Thus, from a payment system perspective, the ICD-9 code set is used is two different ways:

1. To establish medical necessity for almost all claims
2. To drive payment for inpatient services on the UB-04 claim

ICD-9 and ICD-10 are both extensive code sets with complicated coding guidelines. In some cases these guidelines are intertwined with the Medicare inpatient payment system Diagnosis-Related Groups (DRGs). This code set is updated each year on October 1. As with the other major code sets used for healthcare payment, there are many changes each year. When the United States goes to ICD-10, or we may possibly go directly to ICD-11, this will constitute a major change and coding staff will need to be significantly re-educated. Also, ICD-10 uses a seven-alphanumeric format. The HIPAA TSC rule has already required the accommodation of the longer format.

Here are some simple examples of diagnosis codes:

- 250.0—Diabetes mellitus without mention of complication (requires fifth digit)
- 308.0—Predominant disturbance of emotions
- 440.0—Atherosclerosis of aorta
- 663.00—Abdominal pregnancy without intrauterine pregnancy
- V60.3—Person living alone
- E920.0—Accident caused by power lawn mower

Revenue Codes for the UB-04

Revenue codes represent a rather extensive set of codes that are used on the UB-04 claim form to indicate the location or type of service. These codes are officially developed and maintained by the National Uniform Billing Committee (NUBC).* These codes have been developed historically as various needs have arisen so that this code set may appear to be somewhat disorganized. There are families of codes. These are four-digit codes although you will often see the leading zero dropped in casual discussions.

Here are some very brief examples.

002X Health Insurance—Prospective Payment System (HIPPS)

This code indicates the type of classification assignment.

- 0020 Reserved
- 0021 Reserved

---

* See http://www.nubc.org.

- 0022 Skilled Nursing Facility prospective payment system
- 0023 Home health prospective payment system
- 0024 Inpatient rehabilitation facility prospective payment system

The 002X sequence of revenue codes is used for three special Medicare prospective payment systems, namely for Skilled Nursing Facilities (SNFs), Home Health Agencies (HHAs), and Inpatient Rehabilitation Facilities (IRFs).

Here is a sequence used by hospitals with emergency departments:

045X Emergency Room (ER)

This code indicates charges for emergency treatment to ill and injured persons who require immediate unscheduled medical or surgical care.

- 0450 General
- 0451 EMTALA emergency medical screening services
- 0452 ER beyond EMTALA screening
- 0456 Urgent care
- 0459 Other ER

This sequence of revenue codes shows some of the common characteristics present in most sequences, along with some very special instructions. Typically, the top-level revenue code, in this case 0450, is a general category. The last revenue code, 0459, is similar to other sequences in that the revenue code ending in a "9" is for the "other" category and this revenue code should be used only if there are specific instructions to use it. This guidance is typically from a TPP using the revenue code in some unusual way.

For the 045X sequence there are three other revenue codes that should be used only under specific guidance from TPPs. The sequence has been established to allow a hospital to report that there was an Emergency Medical Treatment and Active Labor Act (EMTALA) screening examination (as required by law) using 0451 and then that *either* further emergency services were provided (revenue code 0452) or urgent care (i.e., non-emergent) was provided. This is indicated by using revenue code 0456.

Here is another sequence of revenue codes, this time describing professional services.

096X Professional Fees (see also 097X and 098X)

This code indicates charges for medical professionals when the institutional healthcare provider, along with the payer, require the professional component to be separately identified on the UB-04. This is generally used by Critical Access Hospitals (CAHs) that bill both the technical and professional components on the UB-04 form.

- 0960—General
- 0961—Psychiatric
- 0962—Ophthalmology
- 0963—Anesthesiologist (MD)
- 0964—Anesthetist (CRNA)
- 0969—Other professional fees

This sequence of revenue codes is augmented by two other sequences, 097X and 098X. For instance, ER physicians claiming professional services on the UB-04 would use revenue code 0981. These revenue code sequences allow for billing professional services of various types on the UB-04. The description in this case indicates that these revenue codes are often used by CAHs using the Method II payment approach under a cost-based payment system.

Obviously, we have only given a few examples of hundreds of revenue codes. Healthcare providers filing claims using the UB-04 use these codes. Careful study of these codes and their proper use takes significant effort. Generally this code set is not well organized and is sometimes difficult to understand.

Condition Codes for the UB-04

Condition codes are two-alphanumeric codes used in Form Locators (FLs) 18-28 on the UB-04. The equivalent electronic format, the 837-I, allows much more space for these codes. Up to 11 codes can be reported. The range and application of codes is significant. Here are a few examples:

Condition Code 21—Billing for Denial Notice

This code indicates that the provider realizes that the services are noncovered or excluded from coverage, but requests a denial notice from Medicare to bill the claim to Medicaid or another payer.

Condition Code 22—Patient on Multiple Drug Regimen

This code indicates that the patient is receiving multiple intravenous (IV) drugs while on home IV therapy.

Condition Code 27—Patient Referred to a Sole Community Hospital (SCH) for a Diagnostic Laboratory Test

This code is only to be reported by SCHs. It indicates that the patient was referred for a diagnostic laboratory test.

Condition Code 44—Inpatient Admission Changed to Outpatient

This code is used on outpatient claims only when the physician ordered inpatient services, but upon internal utilization review performed before the claim was originally submitted, the hospital determined that the services did not meet its inpatient criteria.

Condition Code 80—Home Dialysis—Nursing Facility

This code indicates that the billing is for a patient that receives dialysis services at home and that the patient's home is a nursing facility.

Even from this brief set of examples, you can discern that there are many codes addressing various types of situations. Some of these codes are specific to certain TPPs and then to specific payment systems.

As with the revenue codes, the official code set maintainer is the NUBC. However, there are cases in which a specific payer may demand more stringent criteria for allowing a given condition code. A good example is with Condition Code 44.

Condition Code 44 as listed above is to allow a hospital to change the status of an admission from an inpatient admission to an outpatient observation admission if the hospital determines the admission did not meet inpatient admission criteria. This determination must be made before the claim is filed. However, the Medicare program demands significantly more stringent criteria to be met before this code can be used. For the Medicare program, the criteria are:

- The change in admission status from inpatient to outpatient is made prior to discharge or release while the patient is still a patient of the hospital.
- The hospital has not submitted a Medicare claim for the inpatient admission.
- A physician agrees with the utilization review committee's decision.
- The physician documents his or her agreement with the utilization review committee decision in the patient's medical record.

If you read these criteria carefully, you will note that the physician has to agree and the patient must still be in the hospital.

There are many more condition codes and several associated code sets include occurrence codes and value codes.

Place of Service Codes for the 1500

The 1500 claim form is generally used for professional billing and claims filing; however, this claim form is also used by Ambulatory Surgical Centers (ASCs) and Independent Diagnostic Testing Facilities (IDTFs), among others. The various code sets used with this claim form are under the control of the National Uniform Claims Committee (NUCC),* which is the standard code set maintainer under the HIPAA TSC rule for these code sets.

One piece of information that must be provided is the place of service (POS). Interestingly enough, this code set appears to be maintained by CMS as opposed to the NUCC. Although all TPPs can use this code set, the proper POS is particularly important to the Medicare program. Here are a few examples:

■ 11 Office: Location (other than a hospital, SNF, military treatment facility, community health center, state or local public health clinic, or intermediate care facility) where the health professional routinely provides health examinations, diagnoses, and treatment of illness or injury on an ambulatory basis.

■ 15 Mobile Unit: A facility/unit that moves from place to place and is equipped to provide preventive, screening, diagnostic, and/or treatment services.

■ 20 Urgent Care Facility: Location (distinct from a hospital ER, an office, or a clinic) for which the purpose is to diagnose and treat illness or injury for unscheduled, ambulatory patients seeking immediate medical attention.

■ 21 Inpatient Hospital: A facility (other than psychiatric) that primarily provides diagnostic, therapeutic (both surgical and non-surgical), and rehabilitation services by (or under) the supervision of physicians to patients admitted for a variety of medical conditions.

---

* See http://www.nucc.org.

■ 22 Outpatient Hospital: A portion of a hospital that provides diagnostic, therapeutic (both surgical and non-surgical), and rehabilitation services to sick or injured persons who do not require hospitalization or institutionalization.
■ 23 ER—Hospital: A portion of a hospital where emergency diagnoses and treatment of illness or injury are provided.
■ 24 ASC: A freestanding facility (other than a physician's office) where surgical and diagnostic services are provided on an ambulatory basis

The POS codes are available for use by all TPPs using the 1500 claim form. For the Medicare program, there is an additional piece of data that is critically important, namely whether or not the POS code is considered to be a "facility" or "non-facility." In Chapters 3 and 4 we briefly discussed provider-based clinics under Medicare. Hospitals, the main provider, can establish provider-based clinics that can, overall, generate more reimbursement that the same clinic organized as freestanding. When a physician or practitioner provides services in a provider-based clinic (i.e., a facility), then the POS indicator drives a reduction in payment to a physician or practitioner. This is the site-of-service (SOS) differential.

Thus, for the Medicare program, each of these POS numbers also carries a facility or non-facility designation. As might be expected, POS indicators such as 24, 23, 22, and 21 are designated as facility; however, POS 20 for urgent care is classified as non-facility even though the word "facility" appears in the title. Thus, if a hospital has a provider-based urgent care facility, then the POS 22 must still be used.

Standard Transaction Formats

The HIPAA TSC established several standard transaction formats. These generally fall under the ASC X12N standards. Here is a brief listing:

■ Health claims
  – Institutional—ASC X12 N Healthcare Claim (837-I)
  – Professional—ASC X12N Healthcare Claim (837-P)
■ Enrollment and disenrollment in a health plan
  – ASC X12N Benefit Enrollment and Maintenance (834)
■ Eligibility for a health plan
  – See ASC X12N 270 and 271

■ Healthcare payment and remittance advice
  – ASC X12N Healthcare Claim Payment/Advice (835)
■ Healthcare premium payments
  – See ASC X12N 811 and 820
■ Health claim status
  – See ASC X12N 276 and 277
■ Referral certification and authorization
  – ASC X12N Healthcare Service Review Information (278)
■ Coordination of benefits
  – See Form 837

Each of these standard formats has an extensive set of computer specifications that involve hundreds of pages of technical information. From a payment system perspective, our main interest is to make certain that our claims and other transmissions faithfully follow the technical specifications. The ability of a hospital, clinic, or other healthcare provider to meet these various formats is embedded in the billing systems. In many cases healthcare providers may also use clearinghouses to further process their claims to make certain that all of the standards are being met.

The development of these claims transactions is an ongoing process so that coding, billing, and reimbursement personnel for all types of healthcare providers must constantly update themselves and their computer systems that bill and generate claims.

Note: The TSC code sets establish a base level for coding, billing, and filing claims. If a healthcare provider is filing a claim with a private TPP with whom the provider has no relationship, then the general rules and specifications with the HIPAA TSC apply. If the provider is filing a claim with a payer with whom the provider has a contract, then the contract may further specify how the code sets and claims are to be filed. If the claim is being filed with a statutorily established payment system for Medicare, Medicaid, or another governmental payer, then all of the federal and state rules and regulations also come into play.

We have generally referred to the 1500 and UB-04 claims forms for our discussions. However, technically we should be referring to the 837-P and 837-I transaction standards.

The basic concept behind this standardization is to allow for EDI. Figures 6.1 and 6.2 show the types of information flow that can and/or should occur. Presuming that this can be accomplished electronically, that the standard

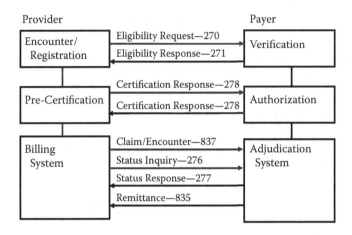

Figure 6.1 Transactions flows with EDI.

formats are used, and that all of the necessary information from the standard code sets is provided, the claims adjudication processing should be very quick at the primary and secondary claim levels.

Figure 6.1 shows an idealized flow using EDI. Because standard transaction formats and standard code sets are utilized, the sequence of events for filing a claim, having the claim adjudicated, and then receiving payment should be accomplished very quickly and with great efficiency.

Figure 6.2 shows the same flow when there is a secondary TPP involved. The crossover claim should occur automatically, again with EDI.

What Figures 6.1 and 6.2 illustrate is a brief insight into EDI. In theory, a provider should be able to provide services, develop the claim, file the

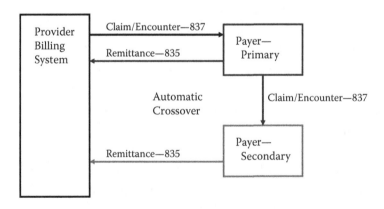

Figure 6.2 Secondary claim automatic crossover.

claim electronically, and be paid quite rapidly. Of course, everything has to work perfectly for this to happen, but this is the ultimate goal of EDI for the healthcare industry.

National Provider Identifiers—NPIs

A part of the HIPAA administrative simplification was the development of various identification numbers. Although identification numbers for individuals becomes politically sensitive, there was a real need to revise and update the identification numbers of healthcare providers. This has generally been accomplished.

A healthcare provider must enroll through the NPI enumerator. This is generally accomplished electronically. Once an NPI has been assigned, it will remain in effect indefinitely. For simple organizational structuring, the NPI is quite straightforward. In Chapter 3 we discussed the organizational structuring of healthcare providers. Structuring can vary from the very simple, such as a solo physician organized as a sole proprietor, on up to integrated delivery systems with hundreds of different kinds of healthcare providers.

In Chapter 5 we briefly addressed gaining billing privileges with the Medicare program using the various CMS-855 forms. In some respects, the NPI process is a simplified version of the CMS-855 process. For instance, our solo physician whose business organization is a sole proprietorship will have a single NPI. The NPI will be for the physician as an individual and also for the business, which is a sole proprietorship. Because there is no distinction between the individual and the business as a sole proprietorship, we will have a single NPI. However, if we have another physician join our solo physician and they incorporate the practice as a professional corporation, then the NPI situation starts to become a little more complicated. Each physician will need an individual NPI and the business, which is now a corporation, will also need to have an NPI.

For large, multifaceted organizations, the way in which the NPIs are gained can vary quite significantly. An organization can designate subunits, which can also obtain NPIs. Thus, in more complex organizational settings, determining the number of NPIs relative to the organizational structuring may require some careful thought. As with the CMS-855 forms, someone must be assigned to handle the NPIs because they may need to be updated from time to time.

HIPAA Security

The implementation of the HIPAA Security Rule lagged behind the privacy and transaction standards. Implementation finally occurred on April 21, 2005. In a surprising move, the final rule was narrowed to address only Electronic Protected Health Information (EPHI). Because this rule was narrowed to just EPHI, the question of security for non-electronic Protected Health Information (PHI) reverted back to the HIPAA Privacy Rule.

A very succinct comparison of the privacy and security rules appears in the February 20, 2003 *Federal Register* on page 8335.

1. The security standards below define **administrative, physical, and technical safeguards** to protect the **confidentiality, integrity, and availability** of electronic protected health information. The standards require covered entities to implement basic safeguards to protect electronic protected health information from unauthorized access, alteration, deletion, and transmission.
2. The Privacy Rule, by contrast, sets standards for how protected health information should be controlled by setting forth what uses and disclosures are authorized or required and what rights patients have with respect to their health information. (68 FR 8335)

For payment systems, the HIPAA Security Rule has an indirect impact. Hospitals, clinics, and other healthcare providers are required to meet certain standards for computers, networks, and telecommunications in general. Some of these standards are mandatory, while others are simply addressable. The HIPAA Security Rule is in the domain of information technology. For coding, billing, and reimbursement (i.e., the reimbursement cycle), the main concern is with secure storage of information and secure telecommunications of PHI.

The HIPAA Security Rule applies only to EPHI. The trigger for the HIPAA Security Rule to apply is electronic storage and/or transmittal of PHI. In the current world of electronic computer systems and telecommunication, this means that the HIPAA Security Rule applies to virtually all healthcare providers of almost any type and also to all TPPs.

Summary and Conclusion

The HIPAA legislation from 1996 definitely affects healthcare providers and all TPPs. The impact on the various payment systems is sometimes peripheral and at the same time very real. On the surface, the HIPAA Privacy Rule would not seem to affect payment systems and the payment process, but, by definition, the designated record set includes various financial information that occurs with billing and claims filing. The HIPAA Security Rule has a peripheral impact as well. The requirements under this part of HIPAA are quite technical and involve maintaining the confidentially of EPHI. Thus, one of the main concerns is security in telecommunications when filing claims and receiving payments (including remittance advice) from the claims.

The HIPAA TSC has a much more direct impact. This rule establishes standard code sets and standard transaction formats. Basically, this allows for EDI in the healthcare field. For our purposes, this is of interest for filing claims and receiving payments. The HIPAA TSC establishes a base level for filing claims. There may also be special TPP requirements that go beyond the requirements within the standards specifications. However, over time the use of the standard code sets and standard claims formats should give much greater efficiency within the reimbursement cycle for the various payment systems.

The NPIs also assist in identifying all of the players in providing healthcare services and/or in paying for such services. Although the organizational structuring of healthcare providers can complicate the issuance and maintenance of the NPIs, at least everyone can know the identity of providers and payers.

Chapter 7

Compliance

Introduction

Whenever a third-party payer (TPP) makes payment for healthcare services, there will always be compliance concerns. Payers will pay if the patient is covered by a given plan, the services rendered or items provided are covered, the services/items are medically necessary for care, the services/care are ordered and provided by qualified medical persons, the care is properly documented, and the claim is correctly and timely filed. Although all of these are conceptually reasonable, the process of ensuring compliance for healthcare payment and the many different types of healthcare payment systems becomes extremely complicated.

We will discuss several compliance issues and associated compliance concepts. Compliance for healthcare payment generally falls into two categories:

1. Statutory compliance: Medicare, Medicaid, Tricare, and other government programs
2. Contractual compliance: Private TPPs, such as insurance carriers and managed care organizations

As we discussed in Chapter 5 when addressing the claims filing process, there is really a third level, that is a base or default compliance level. This base level occurs when a healthcare provider files a claim to a private payer with which there is no relationship (i.e., there is no contractual relationship). We previously referred to this as a general level.

We will look at all three levels, that is, statutory, contractual, and general. In this discussion we will tie together concepts discussed in all of the preceding chapters. Note that this discussion should be considered to be an overview of a very large and convoluted area. Readers are encouraged to pursue these topics by referencing *Compliance for Coding, Billing & Reimbursement: A Systematic Approach to Developing a Comprehensive Program*, published by Productivity Press.

Coding, Billing, and Reimbursement Compliance—Overarching Issues

Among the many payment systems and associated claims filing issues, there are three fundamental issues that tend to appear repeatedly, sometimes in a disguised form. These are:

■ Medical necessity
■ Claims filing versus claims payment
■ Supporting documentation

Medical Necessity

Of all of the issues faced by healthcare providers through the multitude of payment systems, there is always the question, "Were the services provided or items supplied really medically necessary for the care of the patient?" Medical necessity is a judgment issue and is subjective. Because of this subjectivity, disagreements often arise between healthcare providers (and possibly patients) and TPPs. For payment systems that are fee-for-service oriented, the TPP wants services minimized to only those services that are really necessary. For capitated payment processes, the healthcare provider may decide not to provide a service or provide an item in order to save on expenses. In this case the TPP may be lobbying for a service to be provided because it is medically necessary.

Let us look at two simple examples of this pervasive medical necessity issue.

CASE STUDY 7.1—CAT Scan in the Emergency Department (ED)

An individual* presents to the Apex Medical Center's ED late in the evening. He has had a headache for 3 days. The headache is

---

* The word "individual" is used because if a person is a patient at the hospital the EMTALA (Emergency Medical Treatment and Labor Act) does not apply as such.

slowly getting worse and the individual finally came to the ED. The ED physician does a thorough workup including laboratory testing, various x-rays, and finally even a CAT scan. After the complete workup the final diagnosis is sinus congestion and sinusitis. The patient is directed to obtain an over-the-counter decongestant and is sent home.

If you were an insurance company and you reviewed the claim that was generated from this encounter (particularly the final diagnosis), would you question the need to perform an expensive CAT scan? In all fairness to all of the parties involved, this type of diagnostic testing is questionable. Of course, it is easy to question this type of diagnostic test after the fact rather than taking the perspective of the ED physician in not knowing whether there was some more serious condition that needed to be identified.*

Note: Excessive diagnostic testing in the ED has been a longstanding issue. For example, with the Medicare program, the Office of the Inspector General (OIG) has frequently placed this issue in its annual work plans.

CASE STUDY 7.2—Inpatient Admission versus Outpatient Observation

An elderly patient presents to the Apex Medical Center's ED at 9:00 AM. The patient is suffering from general weakness and fatigue, and is just not feeling well. Laboratory tests indicate a severe potassium deficiency. The patient's attending physician is called. The patient had recently been put on a diuretic. However, she refused to take the prescribed potassium supplements. The attending physician admits the patient as an inpatient and orders intravenous infusion of potassium. By the afternoon, the patient is fully recovered. The attending physician assesses the patient and discharges her home.

At first glance, this would appear to be a routine case. Such a potassium deficiency can be life threatening so that the inpatient admission will

---

* As yourself, if it were your child in the ED, would you want any and all diagnostic tests performed to determine the nature and extent of the problem?

generally meet inpatient admission criteria. However, in retrospect, this case really could have been addressed through an observation admission. For the Medicare program there is a significant difference in payment between observation (paid under Ambulatory Payment Classifications [APCs]) and inpatient (paid under Diagnosis-Related Groups [DRGs]). In theory, hospitals have the opportunity to adjust the status of the patient from inpatient to outpatient through the use of a UB-04 Condition Code, namely Code 44.* For the Medicare program this change must occur before the patient is discharged, although this requirement is not present in the official definition of Condition Code 44.

Note: The issue presented in Case Study 7.2 is one of the preeminent issues addressed by the Recovery Audit Contractor (RAC) program as instituted by the Medicare program. Literally tens if not hundreds of millions of dollars are being recovered relative to this subjective medical necessity issue. The basic premise for this issue is that an expensive inpatient stay should not be billed; only a relatively inexpensive observation stay should be billed.

Note that in both of these case studies the medical necessity issue is being judged after the fact. Hindsight is 20/20.

Claims Filing versus Claims Payment

Let us now consider the second issue, which has already been subtlety raised. This is the issue of confusing coding, billing, and claims generation with claim adjudication and payment.

As we discussed in Chapter 5, with the implementation of the HIPAA Transaction Standard/Standard Code Set (TSC) rule, a healthcare provider, for a given service provided and item dispensed, should be able to file a claim in the standard format using standard code sets and then electronically transmit the claim. No matter which TPP is involved, the claim should be the same based upon the services provided. Currently, this goal is still in the distant future.

The basic idea is that the healthcare provider should generate a good, clean, standard claim and then the responsibility for properly adjudicating the claim rests with the TPP. The simple fact is that many TPPs make

---

* Significant controversy has arisen over Condition Code 44 in that the Medicare program has instituted a more stringent definition relative to the official National Uniform Billing Committee (NUBC) definition (see Chapter 6).

unusual demands on the provider when claims are developed and filed. Often these demands to deviate from the norm arise to assist in the adjudication of the claims so filed.

In Case Study 7.2, the hospital may have wanted to change the patient status from inpatient to outpatient observation, but for the Medicare program, if the hospital did not make this change while the patient was still in the hospital, then Condition Code 44 cannot be used. However, the official National Uniform Billing Committee (NUBC) definition for using Condition Code 44 would allow the change to be made even if the patient had been discharged. Thus, the Medicare program has made an unusual demand on the claims filing process to affect proper payment.

Here is another small example of how the coding and billing process can be corrupted by payment systems demands.

CASE STUDY 7.3 — Pre-Operative Antibiotic Injections

At the Apex Medical Center when an outpatient surgical procedure is performed, the surgeons sometimes request that a pre-operative antibiotic injection be provided. This is particularly true with elderly patients or patients whose medical condition requires such an injection. Apex has a TPP that does not want to pay separately for these injections. These injections are considered to be a part of the operative procedure. However, in order not to pay for the injection, Apex must not code and bill for the injections. Otherwise, the payer's adjudication system will pay separately for the injection.

As you can assess from Case Study 7.3, the payer's adjudication system really has the responsibility to pay or not pay for the injection on the basis of the information provided in the claim. The Apex Medical Center's responsibility is to code correctly and bill for the injection and then the claim adjudication process should determine whether separate payment is to be made.

Case Study 7.3 is a simple example of a situation that arises in many different forms. All healthcare providers consume considerable resources to meet special demands of virtually all TPPs, both governmental and private, in order to have the claims properly adjudicated and paid. This is part of the reason why the HIPAA TSC rule was established, that is, to allow healthcare providers to file claims in a standard format consistently using standard code sets.

Supporting Documentation

The old axiom for coding and billing is "If it is not documented, then it was not done." Of course, at a purely logical level this statement is invalid. Services are provided and sometimes not documented. The real question is whether or not the given payment system will reimburse for services provided or items dispensed that are not documented. The resounding answer to this question is "No." From a compliance perspective, the simple fact is that everything must be documented if services are to be billed and paid.

CASE STUDY 7.4—Physician Coding Based on Services, Not Documentation

A recent audit at the Acme Medical Clinic has indicated that one of the physicians appears to be upcoding based on the documentation. This is occurring mainly with office visits that use the evaluation and management (E/M) codes from Current Procedural Terminology (CPT). The physician is interviewed and indicates that there are actually more extensive services being provided but that not everything is being documented. The physician maintains that the code levels are correct based on the actual services, but that it is simply that not everything is documented.

In Case Study 7.4 there is a disconnect in that the physician is coding from what is actually being done versus what is actually being documented. Although this case study illustrates a potentially egregious situation, physicians rarely document everything that they observe, perform, and/or consider when examining a patient. Although the physician absorbs a great deal of information, only certain information is documented. From a payment system perspective, payment will be made only for what is documented.

CASE STUDY 7.5—Cardiovascular Interventional Radiology

The Apex Medical Center is now providing rather extensive coronary and non-coronary vascular interventional radiology services. On the hospital side, the technicians in the catheterization laboratory perform the actual coding for these services on the basis of what they observe the physician perform. A recent audit of the vascular (non-coronary) catheterizations has shown that the coding generated from the observation of services is sometimes quite different from what should have been coded based on the documentation. Also, when the physician's professional claims, which are coded separately, were examined, these claims were again somewhat different.

Again in this case study we have a significant disconnect. What is observed may or may not end up being documented and/or the way in which the documentation is developed may affect the way in which the case should be coded.

Keep in mind that any TPP will only pay for healthcare services if they are medically necessary and properly documented, and the claim is properly coded and billed. Although the services provided must also be for a covered individual and provided by a qualified medical person, the medical necessity, documentation, and proper claim filing are the key compliance issues.

Statutory Compliance

Although there are differences among Medicare, Medicaid, and other governmental programs, as we have demonstrated in other chapters of this book, we will concentrate on the voluminous Medicare rules and regulations.

Rules, Laws, and Information

There is a significant hierarchy of different types and formality of guidance for coding and billing under the Medicare program. Here is a brief categorization, starting with congressional laws and ending with informal Center for Medicare and Medicaid Services (CMS) guidance.

- Social Security Act plus congressional laws
- United States Code
- *Code of Federal Regulations*
- *Federal Register*
- CMS Manual System including transmittals
- *Medicare Learning Network (MLN) Matters* articles
- CMS Medicare Administrative Contractor Guidance
- CMS open forums, roundtable presentations, and questions and answers (Q&As)

Given this extensive hierarchy, there are hundreds of thousands of pages of information and guidance on the ever increasing number of Medicare payment systems. Also, as the different payment systems mature, there is a tendency for a given system to become more complex. Furthermore, given that there are different sources for information and guidance, sometimes ambiguities arise and there can even be conflicting guidance.

At the very top of the hierarchy is the Social Security Act (SSA), which may simply be called "the act." Although the SSA may be cited for reference, most healthcare providers addressing compliance for coding, billing, and associated reimbursement will typically start their study of changes at the *Federal Register* level. All of the Medicare payment systems are updated through an annual *Federal Register* process. Note that this updating process really updates the *Code of Federal Regulations* (CFR). The CFR is official from a legal perspective.

CMS has an extensive set of manuals that provide greater detail for definitions, billing processes, claims filing, and the like. These manuals are updated through an ongoing process of issuing Transmittals on the basis of Change Requests (CRs). Hundreds of sometimes lengthy Transmittals are issued every year. The Transmittals are directed toward the Medicare Administrative Contractors (MACs). Often when a Transmittal is issued, a slightly revised or plain-language *MLN Matters* article is also issued for healthcare providers.

CMS also conducts various open forum meetings on various issues and topics. In these meetings, which are often extended teleconferences, questions can be posed and answers provided. CMS also sometimes issues Q&A documents. Additionally, the MACs themselves also provide guidance in various forms that may include extensive monthly newsletters and memorandums.

From this very brief discussion you can correctly conclude that there is a great volume of guidance that can sometimes be inconsistent. To meet all of the statutory compliance guidance from any single Medicare payment system is a major challenge. Coding, billing, and reimbursement personnel should take the time and effort to develop professional networks of contacts. Additionally, contacts should be developed and maintained with personnel at the appropriate MAC.

Note: Section 921 of the Medicare Modernization Act of 2003 requires the MACs to provide answers to questions in a clear, concise, and accurate manner. The questions should be in writing and the MAC has 45 working days to respond.

Office of the Inspector General

Over the last 15 years the OIG has issued a significant body of compliance guidance for all types of healthcare providers that are involved with the Medicare program and to some extent with the Medicaid programs at the state level. OIG publications include:

- Fraud alerts
- Annual OIG work plan
- *Federal Register* Compliance Program guidance
- Special reports resulting from audits and studies
- Corporate integrity agreements
- Advisory opinions

This is only a partial listing. Anyone who is involved in coding, billing, and associated payment from any of the many Medicare payment systems should routinely visit the OIG website for updated information. The OIG guidance is general, covering all types of compliance issues. However, much of the guidance provided relates to many coding, billing, and reimbursement issues under the various Medicare payment systems.

Major Medicare Rules and Requirements

In other chapters we have discussed Medicare rules and regulations that directly involve coding, billing, and associated payment systems. For instance the CfPs (Conditions for Payment) and the Provider-Based Rule (PBR) have a significant, direct impact relative to healthcare payment. Many of the other major rules, regulations, and associated processes can involve payment systems to some extent.

For instance, Emergency Medical Treatment and Labor Act (EMTALA) is a law that indirectly involves payment systems such as APCs. However, decisions must be made in meeting the various rules and regulations surrounding EMTALA coding and billing. Consider situations in which an individual presents to an ED, the patient is triaged, and diagnostic tests are performed by standing order. However, the individual then leaves before the mandated medical screening examination (MSE) can be performed. Can the diagnostic tests legitimately be billed?

Another major compliance area is the Medicare Conditions of Participation (CoPs). There is a slightly different version of CoPs for Critical Access Hospitals (CAHs). Regardless of the type of hospital, care must be given to considering any coding, billing, and associated payment systems concerns that might arise.

Recovery Audit Contractor Audits

The Recovery Audit Contractor (RAC) program has been developed and implemented by the Medicare program. Most of the issues addressed by the RAC audits are not new. Generally all of the issues have been identified by the OIG, Medicare audits, and/or investigations by the U.S. Department of Justice (DOJ). What is new with the RAC audits is the extent to which these audits will be conducted. Virtually every healthcare provider will be scrutinized to some extent by the RAC audits.

The incentive for the RAC auditors is that the auditing companies are paid on a contingency basis. The more overpayments that they find, the more money they, the RAC auditors, make. Medical necessity is one of the overarching compliance concerns and this is a subjective issue. Thus compliance takes on a very new meaning in that there can be differences of opinion in what is medically justified or not. Case Study 7.2 provides an illustration of this particular type of issue. Here is another case study illustrating the subjectivity of medical necessity determinations.

CASE STUDY 7.6—3-Day Inpatient Qualifying Stay Prior to SNF Admission

Under the Medicare program, a beneficiary must have a 3-day qualifying stay as an inpatient for a SNF admission to be covered. The Apex Medical Center has just conducted an audit and discovered that 90% of their knee replacement procedures had exactly a 3-day inpatient stay with an admission to a SNF.

If you were a RAC auditor reviewing cases, do you think this type of statistic would raise a red flag?

Correct coding and proper documentation are always issues. RAC auditors use data mining techniques to analyze claim and coding patterns. If aberrations or suspicious patterns arise, then further investigation may result in direct review of selected cases.

Our third overarching compliance concern discussed above was the confusion between claims filing and the adjudication and payment of claims. This same challenge exists with the RAC audits. A healthcare provider may develop, code, and file a claim using guidance from the Medicare program. The MAC may adjudicate the claim and actually make payment. Under normal circumstances this would appear to complete the transaction. However, a review of certain types of cases may reveal that the MAC incorrectly paid the claim even though all current policies were followed. In cases of this type the RAC auditors will still want to recoup the overpayment that has resulted. In some cases a given situation may require CMS to develop more explicit guidance.

Consider Case Study 7.3 involving pre-operative antibiotic injections. In theory these injections are separately codeable and billable. The MAC in adjudicating the claim may even pay separately for them. But at a later time a review may be made and the assertion may be made that such injections should not have been separately paid because they were really a part of the surgery payment.

Even with this brief discussion, the RAC audits will present some very real challenges for almost all healthcare providers involved with the Medicare program and thus statutory compliance.

Contractual Compliance

Contractual compliance is distinctly different from statutory compliance in that the needed information is not necessarily publicly available. You may need to seek out the needed information to code, bill, and be reimbursed under a contractual arrangement. In theory, the contract that is negotiated and signed by a healthcare provider with a TPP should be comprehensive. However, the contract may be relatively brief with references to various companion manuals, websites, and/or other sources of information.

Coding, billing, and reimbursement personnel may need to affirmatively seek out information. Sometimes contracts are negotiated and signed without review of coding and billing personnel. The way in which payment is to be made can and does affect the way coding and billing are performed. Thus when contracts are established there should be appropriate review of the contract itself along with any additional guidance for coding, billing, and associated payment.

CASE STUDY 7.7—Implants versus Supplies

The Apex Medical Center has a fee-for-service contract with a local insurance company. The hospital is paid on a percentage of charges, but the actual percentage varies according to revenue code. Supply items under revenue code 0272 are paid at 50% whereas items under revenue code 0278, other implants, are paid at 80%.

Given this basic information relative to payment, do you think there might be some compliance concerns relative to proper classification of supply items?

CASE STUDY 7.8—Contract Gap

The Apex Medical Center has a rather extensive contractual arrangement with a local insurance company. A situation has just arisen that was not covered in the contract. Under the contract, Apex is paid on a per diem basis for inpatient services. Apex does not provide skilled nursing services. A patient was recently in the hospital and when the attending physician discharged the patient, the discharge was to a skilled nursing level of service. However, there were no skilled nursing beds available in the community. The patient stayed in his inpatient bed for an additional 4 days before a SNF bed became available. The contractual arrangement had no provision for paying for such services.

Gaps in contractual arrangements are not that uncommon. Even the Medicare program for the DRG payment system has guidance on this particular case study in that the patient remains an inpatient and payment is through the DRG payment. The important point with these gaps is to have a way for the healthcare providers and TPPs to quickly get together and resolve any such issues or gaps. In some contracts the process for resolution may be addressed explicitly in the contract.

Healthcare providers must constantly monitor the reimbursement being received through the many different contracts and associated payment systems. Although healthcare providers have contractual obligations, the TPPs also must meet their obligations. One way to carefully assess whether contractual relations are really working is to monitor reimbursement. If the expected reimbursement was not received, then there may be a problem. Perhaps the claim was not properly coded or the billing was incorrect. On the other hand, there may have been some sort of change on the TPP side.

CASE STUDY 7.9—Sudden Reduction in Payment

The Apex Medical Center has a fee-for-service contract with a TPP that pays 90% of whatever is charged. Reimbursement under this contract has been very good with few discrepancies. However, recently the claims that have been filed with venipuncture charges of $10 are not being paid the 90%, or $9. It appears that the charges are simply being dropped.

The basic facts in Case Study 7.9 can arise in many different forms. Healthcare providers must be very watchful for any changes or variations in payment. If there is a sudden drop in payment, and/or codes are not being recognized, and/or charges are being dropped, and/or any number of other aberrations, then questions should immediately be raised with the given TPP. Particularly with contract relations, having appropriate contacts at the given TPP becomes paramount.

For this case study an investigation and inquiry to the TPP may result in the fact that the payer implemented a new policy of bundling the venipuncture charge into the various laboratory charges. However, this policy change may not have been intended for a percentage-of-charges contract and thus the adjudication policy change was incorrectly applied.

The bottom line is that there is enormous variation in contractual provisions along with dozens if not hundreds of different payment systems. Maintaining contractual compliance is also a major effort for healthcare providers.

Note: Statutory compliance generally is placed at a higher priority than is contractual compliance. The simple reasoning is that statutory compliance has the potential to generate criminal prosecutions as well as civil litigation. Both levels must be addressed. One of the best ways to address compliance for coding, billing, and reimbursement is to fully understand the payment systems involved.

Beyond Statutory and Contractual Compliance

Although the main classifications for coding, billing, and reimbursement compliance generally involves statutory compliance for programs such as Medicare and then contractual compliance with a wide variety of private TPPs, there is also a general or default compliance level. This default level occurs when a healthcare provider files a claim with a TPP with which there is no relationship. In some sense, the claims are filed blindly with the healthcare provider not knowing how the claim will be adjudicated, whether there are any special claims filing requirements, and exactly how or whether the claim will be paid.

With the implementation of the HIPAA TSC rule and the universal use of National Provider Identifiers (NPIs), there is a defined default or base level of compliance that must be maintained through these standard claims formats and various standard code sets. For instance, physicians coding and filing claims for office visits use the CPT E/M codes. These codes are typically in a series of levels. For an established patient office visit the five levels are 99211–99215. For the Medicare program, physicians have rather extensive documentation guidelines that go beyond what is provided in the American Medical Association (AMA)'s CPT manual. However, the default guidance for E/M-level coding lies with the AMA, which is the standard code set maintainer for the CPT coding system.

Thus a physician filing a claim with a private TPP with whom there is no contractual relationship would only be under the compliance requirements as stated within the use of the standard code sets and standard claim formats. Even with this base level there can be severe compliance considerations.

CASE STUDY 7.10 — Solo Specialist Physician Upcoding

Dr. Tyrone is a solo specialist with a clinic in Anywhere, USA. Dr. Tyrone has opted out* of the Medicare program and also has no contractual agreements with any managed care and/or insurance companies. Dr. Tyrone is surprised to learn that the DOJ is investigating and considering filing charges of mail fraud relative to upcoding E/M levels of service.

Thus, even this baseline of standard code sets and standard claim formats form compliance requirements that can actually result in criminal prosecutions.

Establishing a Coding, Billing, and Reimbursement Compliance Program

Every healthcare provider should develop a formal, written compliance plan. The compliance plan will cover more than just payment issues. Areas such as the Occupational Safety and Health Administration (OSHA), the U.S.

---

* Physicians and practitioners can opt out of the Medicare program. They can still see Medicare patients, but the patients are under a private contract, the patient must pay, and the physician does not file claims with Medicare.

Environmental Protection Agency (EPA), the Americans with Disabilities Act (ADA), and the Fair Labor Standards Act (FLSA) represent a small sampling of more general issues that must be addressed by almost any business organization including healthcare providers.

Over the past 2 decades there has been significant activity with healthcare compliance surrounding various fraud and abuse issues. For statutory compliance, criminal penalties can arise as well as civil monetary penalties. Seven basic principles have been developed to mitigate criminal sentences as a result of various criminal prosecutions. In other words, if these principles were appropriately implemented and maintained, then the criminal sentences could be reduced. These seven principles in shortened form are:

1. Compliance standards and procedures
2. Oversight responsibilities
3. Delegation of authority
4. Employee training
5. Monitoring and auditing
6. Enforcement and discipline
7. Response and prevention

We can take these seven principles and apply them to the coding, billing, and reimbursement world that involves the many different healthcare payment systems. Although all of them are important, there are three that are preeminent.

Written Policies and Procedures

Healthcare providers who file claims with many different TPPs and are paid under a multitude of different payment systems must make numerous decisions when filing claims. Although there are supposed to be standard ways to document, code, and bill, even the TPPs themselves may make unusual demands relative to claim filing. The Medicare program has thousands of pages of rules and regulations with ambiguous and sometimes conflicting guidance. One form of protection is to carefully develop written policies and procedures to document what decisions have been made and why they were made.

Employee Training

Employees in the coding and billing world typically want to do things in a proper fashion that ensures correct payment. Those providing healthcare services want to provide the best services possible and also to properly document what they did and why. A key issue for compliance is that everyone needs to know exactly what it is that they should be doing or, sometimes, not doing. The only real way to do this is to take payment systems guidance along with the written policies and procedures and to then provide extensive, ongoing training. Such training in and of itself must also be documented for compliance purposes.

Monitoring and Auditing

In the coding, billing, and reimbursement area auditing is a routine process. There are all kinds of audits ranging from an informal probe audit to formal audits that may go back several years. Although audits can be classified in many different ways, here is a fairly simple classification:

- Prospective
- Concurrent
- Retrospective

Prospective audits concentrate on the systems and processes that are used to develop and file claims including reimbursement monitoring. Concurrent audits address both of the systems and processes along with a review of current claims, that is, generally claims no more that 90 days old. Retrospective audits are generally formal claims audits that can go back several years.

Each of these types of general audits has advantages and disadvantages. The concurrent audits are nice because if there are problems found with the claims, the claims can be corrected and refiled. Retrospective audits carry the burden that overpayments may be discovered for which there is no opportunity to refile and correct the claims. In these cases, repayment may need to be made.

Although there is a great deal of emphasis on written policies and procedures, and then also documenting various compliance activities, healthcare compliance relative to payment is a very dynamic and ever changing area; thus, a compliance plan must also be dynamic. One of the great difficulties is that although compliance personnel must address currently known issues, being able to forecast what will be an issue in several years is of much more value. It is today that we can address issues that will become areas of focus in the future.

Summary and Conclusion

Compliance for coding, billing, and reimbursement under a myriad of different payment systems is a major topic. A framework for further study and analysis has been provided in this chapter. The most serious compliance issues surround the governmental programs, particularly Medicare and Medicaid. The associated compliance issues are serious because not only can there be civil monetary penalties, there can also be criminal prosecutions. Compliance through various contractual obligations is still of concern. However, disagreements and failure to meet obligations generally are resolved with civil arbitration and civil litigation.

Every healthcare provider must establish a compliance program. A major part of any such program must deal with coding, billing, and reimbursement under a multitude of payment systems. Although there are general overarching compliance issues, each specific type of healthcare provider will also have certain areas and specific situations that are special to the specific type of healthcare provider.

Chapter 8

Research, Problem Solving, and Knowledge-Base Development

Introduction

There are many different types of healthcare providers, healthcare providers are organized in many different ways, and there are hundreds, if not thousands, of different payment mechanisms for healthcare services. For personnel involved in the reimbursement cycle, anything and everything needs to be known about each payment system that is being used to provide payment to the given healthcare provider. This includes documentation requirements, prior authorizations, notices of non-coverage, coding, billing, charging, and various claims filing requirements. We have also discussed the need to be fully aware of claims adjudication processes and idiosyncrasies that are embedded in the overall payment process.

Even for a modestly sized healthcare provider, perhaps a small physician clinic, the amount of information that must be acquired, organized, analyzed, and then properly utilized is almost overwhelming. If we move the healthcare provider up into the range of a small integrated delivery system, the volume of information increases exponentially.

We will take a brief look at some of the challenges involved in performing research and knowledge-base development. Two different perspectives will be taken. First we will look at general healthcare payment system knowledge bases. To some degree these general knowledge bases are available commercially. The downside is that such knowledge bases can only really address the statutorily defined payment systems, namely Medicare, Medicaid, and associated governmental programs. This means that for your commercial or private payers you will need to establish separate databases of information. Note that much of the needed information may be accessible through the Internet or sometimes more limited intranets.

The second level is more of a personal knowledge base that you will pull together over the years as you work with the reimbursement cycle within your organization. Although your specific work may specialize within certain payer types and thus within certain payment systems, you will still need to have ready access to various documents and information. Retrieving a document from four years ago may be a real challenge. Also, you will often use some sort of third-party payer (TPP) guidance as the basis for developing coding and billing policies and procedures. When this occurs, be certain to save the documentation providing the guidance within your own personal knowledge base. Information that is available through the Internet or an intranet may not be available at a later date.

In addition to being able to gather, organize, and update significant quantities of information, you must also be able to solve problems. Generally, the problems encountered with payment systems occur someplace within the overall reimbursement cycle. We looked at the reimbursement cycle in Chapter 4 in general terms. For your specific situation you will need to drill down into the many subprocesses that are involved in the reimbursement cycle for your particular type or types of healthcare providers. There may be coding issues, billing issues, charging issues, and claim generation issues, and the list can go on at some length.

Overarching all of our efforts are the many compliance concerns that we discussed in Chapter 7. Although certain payment systems have common elements and mechanisms, we must constantly go back to the fundamentals of covered individual, covered services, medically necessary, ordered by a physician, and fully documented. Then, of course, we have to charge, bill, and code the claim correctly according to general requirements and, possibly, special requirements, from the given payer.

Systematic Process for Knowledge Management

A systematic process of developing a knowledge base, both those that are commercially available and then your own personal knowledge base, is to consider these steps:

- ■ Acquire
- ■ Organize
- ■ Analyze and assess
- ■ Use

For commercial knowledge bases, the acquisition and organization of the information is predetermined by the vendor of the knowledge base. With your personal knowledge base you will need to consider these steps on your own.

Acquiring Information

Sometimes you have too much information and other times you have too little. For the statutorily based payment systems, such as Diagnosis-Related Groups (DRGs), Ambulatory Payment Classifications (APCs), and Resource-Based Relative Value Systems (RBRVS), you may well have more information than you can handle. Given the *Federal Register* process for any of the major payment systems, along with the various manuals, and you have a recipe for an overabundance of information. The challenge in these cases is to sort through all of the information to determine that which is relevant and applicable to your specific situation.

If we go to the contractual payment systems (i.e., payment systems in which your healthcare provider has a negotiated contract) you may find that you have to request information or otherwise seek out relevant information. You may even find yourself in the position of needing to request and justify access to the actual contract itself.

At the compliance level, you will find significant amounts of information through the Office of the Inspector General (OIG) and associated Medicare compliance guidance. At the contractual level, the key elements should be in the contract or companion manuals or other sources of information referenced in the contracts themselves.

An important set of skills in our world of technology is the use of the Internet to conduct research. You may also find that you will be using a variation of the Internet, or what is called an intranet. Intranets use Internet technology, but there is significantly increased limitation to access. For instance, you may have a contract with a private payer that allows you access to the payer's intranet to gain information about claims filing and billing.

Be certain to hone your skills in conducting searches, understanding the use of keywords, and then, particularly for the Internet, keeping a list of websites where you can obtain information. There are many different sources. The Center for Medicare and Medicaid Services (CMS) maintains a very large website that requires some time and effort to use effectively. There are also many healthcare specialty organizations that have information about coding and billing in specialized areas.

Organizing Information

The way in which you organize your personal knowledge base is really up to you. In general, you will want to keep your own personal copies of important documents. For instance, the Medicare website is an excellent source of information. You may find a question-and-answer document that provides useful information. You may even develop a billing policy on the basis of this information. However, several years down the road you may need to access this document only to find that it is no longer on the Medicare website. Thus, you need to save your own copies of important documents that you use for establishing procedures.

If you are involved with multiple payment systems and multiple TPPs, then one way to organize your knowledge base is to sort on the TPP and then sort on the specific payment system being used. Additionally, you may need to separate coding issues from billing issues from claim filing issues from compliance issues. In other words, give some time and thought as to how you organize all of this information, including documents to which you save pointers versus information for which you save the actual documents, which may include grabbing actual websites to keep as a reference.

Note: When organizing your knowledge base, you may need to save multiple copies of the same document classified in two or more ways. This can help in retrieving important documents. For instance, you may work with several different kinds of non-physician practitioners (NPPs). Some of the Medicare guidance for NPPs may include more than one type. However, you may want to save the document, perhaps a transmittal, under each of the different types of NPPs affected.

Most professionals working with the reimbursement cycle for various healthcare providers will generally organize information using some sort of a folder-driven file structure. You decide how to structure the information and then organize your folders and subfolders accordingly. For advanced users, you may also want to develop an indexing system of some sort. This requires quite a bit of skill but can be worth the effort. When you are using commercial knowledge bases you may not only be able to do keyword searches, but you may have access to sophisticated indexing systems as well.

Analyzing and Assessing Information

You will find yourself doing a lot of reading. For paper documents we have those wonderful highlighters that can assist in identifying and organizing key points. In today's electronic environment, you may work more often with MS Word documents or Adobe Acrobat PDF files. We still have highlighting and even commenting capabilities, but you will need to take the time to learn these techniques.

There is no easy way to learn to read the various documents from CMS. In Chapter 7 we listed a whole hierarchy of types of documents starting with the Social Security Act (SSA), working down to informal documents such as open forums held by CMS. Over time, the best approach is to start reading at the more informal level and then work your way up the ladder of formality depending upon your need to understand any one of the different Medicare payment systems.

On the commercial or private TPP side you will not find the depth of different kinds of documents. Here you may find that the information is rather sparse and you may have to learn what really happens to your claims on the basis of the remittance advice being received along with the payment.

Regardless of the particular payer or payment system, you are going to encounter situations and questions for which there appears to be no written answer. This is where you must extend your knowledge base to include personal contacts with representative of the TPP and professional associates.

In theory, representatives of the different payers should be able to answer any questions that you might have. For instance, with the Medicare program the Medicare Modernization Act (MMA) in Section 921 allows you the right to ask specific questions in writing and to obtain clear, concise, and accurate answers from your Medicare Administrative Contractor.

In practice, you may find it difficult to obtain answers to your questions. This is where your professional colleagues can come into play. Often when you encounter a problem, question, or claim adjudication problem, someone else has probably experienced this as well. By developing a network of professional colleagues you can often make some phone calls or send some e-mails to get an answer or at least be pointed in the direction of an answer. In other words, think of your knowledge base as extending beyond your computer system, the Internet, and on out into a professional network of contacts including those at the payers. Keeping your professional network up to date will be a challenge. You may encounter situations in which you have finally identified a person on the payer side that really seems to know what is going on and then he or she is suddenly transferred or changes jobs.

Using the Information

If you have developed your own personal knowledge base or have the luxury of accessing a commercial knowledge base, then using the information generally is not an issue. The big issue is to find and retrieve the information that you need to address a specific problem or situation.

Constant Change

The rate of change for payment systems and the associated processes of coding, billing, claims filing, and reimbursement seems to be accelerating. Depending on the number of different types of payment systems that your healthcare organization must utilize, changes can occur almost on a daily basis. Claims are rejected, claims are underpaid, and claims are delayed because of processing errors. All of these situations are of concern. As discussed in Chapter 5, claims adjudication tracking is really important. Monitoring and analyzing the problems that claims have in progressing through the adjudication process for a given TPP and then the specific payment system being utilized gives healthcare providers the ability to enhance their coding, billing, and thus reimbursement.

The real issue is how to keep up to date with this constant change. There is no simple and certainly no easy answer to this question. We discussed the concept of a knowledge base above and provided some of the sources of information for both a general knowledge base as well as a personal knowledge base. To keep everything current you will need to design a program of study including attending various workshops, teleconferences, presentations, and then also reading the latest pronouncements from your various TPPs.

Systematic Process for Problem Solving

In your professional work dealing with healthcare payment systems you will encounter problems that sometimes seem to defy any reasonable solution.

What you need in your personal toolkit is simply a general problem-solving strategy. One way to resolve problems and challenges is to have a systematic or step-by-step method. Generally, this is called the systems approach. There is no one universal systems approach other than to have a process in which various steps are taken to address problem situations.

Here is a seven-step process that can be used in resolving all kinds of problems, both professional and personal for that matter.

1. Problem identification
2. Problem investigation
3. Problem analysis
4. External solution design
5. Internal solution design
6. Implementation
7. Monitoring and corrective action

There is nothing unusual in this approach. You may wish to use more steps or fewer steps. The trick is to have a template to follow when you encounter problems. In some cases, particularly when dealing with payment systems, the main problem is simply having the proper information to file claims correctly and be properly paid. However, some situations can run much deeper and require a great deal of thought and effort.

The first three steps in this approach are devoted to the problem. This may seem a little unusual, but experience over the years has shown that when we encounter a problem, we may only be looking at the symptoms of the problem and not the real problem. This can be particularly true when you are dealing with a compliance issue within the given payment system or there is suddenly a change in the adjudication process that is not announced.

For instance, through claims adjudication tracking you may notice that certain claims are not being fully paid or, at least, not paid the way they were before. This should be perceived as a problem, but what really is the problem? Is it something that is or is not being done at the time services are provided or billed, or claims developed? Or is this really something that is occurring with the claims adjudication software on the payer's side? Always take the time and effort to determine the real problem.*

---

* See the whole discipline of *root cause analysis.*

Steps 4 and 5 deal with the design of the solution to a problem or possibly improving a process. This has been divided into two parts: the external and internal design. The external solution is the way the solution will look to those using the solution versus the actual internal workings of the solution. This is analogous to our discussion of white-box edits versus black-box edits in Chapter 5. Users of a healthcare billing system often do not care about the internal workings and as long as the proper data are input and the proper bills and claims are generated they are happy. Others may want to know the detailed working of how the fix works, that is, the internals of the solution. Obviously the designers of the solution need to consider both aspects.

Steps 6 and 7 are pretty standard. Implementation can almost be transparent; that is, the personnel involved in various aspects of the reimbursement cycle may not even notice that there has been a change, particularly if the change is to the software in the billing and claims generation software. On the other hand a new documentation requirement, charge capture process, or coding technique may require extensive education and training. Regardless of how complicated the implementation of the solution might be, we must always follow up to make certain that the system is working properly.

Policies and Procedures

Chapter 7 addresses compliance issues surrounding the coding, billing, and reimbursement processes through different payment systems. Because of all of the variations and unusual demands with different TPPs and different payment systems, establishing written policies and procedures is absolutely mandatory. Coding, billing, and reimbursement personnel make decisions almost every day that affect the way bills are developed, claims are filed, and payment is, or sometimes is not, made. These decisions need to be documented with appropriate reference to the guidance that caused the particular decision to be made.

For instance, in Case Study 7.3 we encountered the pre-operative antibiotic injections. As a general default you may have a policy of coding and billing for this service. After all, you did provide the service, you assumed medical-legal liability, and it is generally a codeable and billable service so that your base policy is to code and bill. Now you may have one payer that insists that this injection can be charged separately, but there should be no Current Procedural Terminology (CPT) injection code associated. Another TPP insists that there be no separate charge (or code) and that the charge should be bundled into the associated surgery charge. You may even have another payer that pays for the administration through the drug payment so that there should be no separate charge for the administration.

Thus, each time you alter your billing, coding, and claims filing procedures from the base approach or what should be the norm, be certain to document any and all deviations. Indicate the specific guidance that directs the change from what is considered to be the norm. Given that you will have hundreds, if not thousands, of these types of situations that require you to do something different for individual TPPs, the process of documenting all of these different situations is not trivial.

Now the complexity of coding, billing, and filing claims will depend on the type and size of the healthcare provider for whom you are filing claims. A small physician clinic, a single Home Health Agency operation, or an Independent Diagnostic Testing Facility may encounter fewer situations than would a larger hospital or small integrated delivery system. Large or small, the compliance mandate remains the same: write it up as a policy and procedure.

For instance, in a hospital setting there will be extensive policies and procedures involving coding, billing, and reimbursement issues in areas such as:

- Coding policies and procedures
- Billing policies and procedures
- Chargemaster policies and procedures
- Utilization review policies and procedures

Additionally, the various policies and procedures in each of these areas must dovetail with each other. Also, the billing system along with back-end editing systems must all be coordinated with these policies and procedures.

Summary and Conclusion

In this brief chapter, the need to develop your own personal knowledge base along with possible access to commercial knowledge bases has been discussed. With governmental programs you will probably be overwhelmed with the amount of material that passes your desk. In this case you need to find some way to filter the information so that you can study and assess pertinent information.

For private payers, you may have to go out of your way to identify and access information. In other words, you may be underwhelmed with the lack of material or at least the difficulty of access. Keep in mind that your personal knowledge base should be considered to be more than a computer database of documents. You should expand your thinking to include contacts with personnel at the payer organization and then also to contacts with professional colleagues performing duties similar to your own.

Written policies and procedures are the cornerstone for compliance, along with effective utilization of the reimbursement cycle. The overall goal is to provide high-quality care; generate good, clean claims; and then be properly paid. The only real way to do this is to fully understand the payment system in use, how claims will be adjudicated, and any unusual circumstances to be considered. Every time a decision is made to alter some aspect of the reimbursement cycle to accommodate some directive or requirement on the part of a payer, a written policy and procedure should be developed.

Finally, a fairly simple systematic problem-solving approach was discussed. This seven-step process emphasizes problem identification and separating the solution design into external versus internal aspects. As with any systems approach, the ability to effectively use it lies with the experience and knowledge of those addressing the problems and opportunities.

Appendix I: Case Study Listing

Throughout this book we have used small case studies to illustrate various issues and information provided. This is intended to assist readers in more fully understanding some of the complex and interlaced issues surrounding healthcare payment systems. This appendix provides a listing of the various cases within each of the chapters. Note that in some instances, a given case may be repeated from a different perspective.

Chapter 1

No case studies.

Chapter 2

Case Study 2.1—Minor Automobile Accident
Case Study 2.2—Hospital Services
Case Study 2.3—Hospital Service Additional Payment
Case Study 2.4—Drug Payment
Case Study 2.5—Chargemaster Review
Case Study 2.6—Worker's Compensation TPP
Case Study 2.7—Lesion Excision
Case Study 2.8—Inpatient Pneumonia
Case Study 2.9—Fractured Toe
Case Study 2.10—ED Presentation for Fall
Case Study 2.11—Home Health after Inpatient Stay
Case Study 2.12—Outpatient Surgery—ASC versus Hospital
Case Study 2.13—Capitated Plan
Case Study 2.14—Coronary Stent Placement

Chapter 3

Case Study 3.1—Clinic with Independent Practices
Case Study 3.2—Hospital Clinics and ASC
Case Study 3.3—Office-Based Surgical Procedure Payment
Case Study 3.4—Small Community Hospital
Case Study 3.5—Provider-Based Clinic at the Summit Nursing Facility
Case Study 3.6—Apex Joining to Form an IDS
Case Study 3.7—Orthopedic Specialty Hospital within a Short-Term Acute-
      Care Hospital

Chapter 4

Case Study 4.1—Elderly Patient Accidental Fall
Case Study 4.2—Nonselective Renal Angiography after Heart Catheterization
Case Study 4.3—Inpatient Admission after Outpatient Surgery
Case Study 4.4—Inpatient-Only Surgery Provided as an Outpatient
Case Study 4.5—Durable Medical Equipment to Medicare Hospital Inpatients
Case Study 4.6—Crutches, Canes, and Walkers for ED Patients
Case Study 4.7—Hyperbaric Oxygen to SNF Residents
Case Study 4.8—Physical Therapist Called to ED
Case Study 4.9—DRG Pre-Admission Window

Chapter 5

Case Study 5.1—Delayed Charges
Case Study 5.2—Nurse Practitioner Reassignment
Case Study 5.3—Apex Medical Center Board
Case Study 5.4—Small, Integrated Delivery System
Case Study 5.5—Billing Privileges for Non-Physician Practitioners
Case Study 5.6—Plastic Surgeon Comes to Anywhere, USA
Case Study 5.7—Seeking MAC Guidance on Claim Adjudication
Case Study 5.8—Combination Physical and Occupational Therapy Services
Case Study 5.9—Claims Adjudication Tracking

Chapter 6

No case studies.

Chapter 7

Case Study 7.1—CAT Scan in the Emergency Department (ED)
Case Study 7.2—Inpatient Admission versus Outpatient Observation
Case Study 7.3—Pre-Operative Antibiotic Injections
Case Study 7.4—Physician Coding Based on Services, Not Documentation
Case Study 7.5—Cardiovascular Interventional Radiology
Case Study 7.6—3-Day Inpatient Qualifying Stay Prior to SNF Admission
Case Study 7.7—Implants versus Supplies
Case Study 7.8—Contract Gap
Case Study 7.9—Sudden Reduction in Payment
Case Study 7.10—Solo Specialist Physician Upcoding

Chapter 8

No case studies.

Appendix II: Acronym Listing

This is a list of the more common acronyms that are used in connection with healthcare payment systems. New acronyms and terminology seem to arise almost every day.

1500—Professional Claim Form (see CMS-1500)
6σ—Six Sigma (see Quality Improvement Techniques)

AA—Anesthesia Assistant
A/P—Accounts Payable
A/R—Accounts Receivable
ABC—Activity-Based Costing
ABN—Advance Beneficiary Notice (see also NONC, HINNC)
ACC—Ambulatory Care Center
ACEP—American College of Emergency Physicians
ACHE—American College of Healthcare Executives
ACS—Ambulatory Care Services
ADA—Americans with Disabilities Act
AHA—American Hospital Association
AHIMA—American Health Information Management Association
ALJ—Administrative Law Judge
ALOS—Average Length of Stay
AMA—American Medical Association or American Management Association
AO—Advisory Opinion
AOAA—American Osteopathic Association Accreditation
APC—Ambulatory Payment Classification(s)
AP-DRGs—All Patient DRGs
APG—Ambulatory Patient Group(s)
APR-DRGs—All Patient Refined DRGs
ASC—Ambulatory Surgery Center

ASCII—American Standard Code for Information Interchange
ASF—Ambulatory Surgical Facility
AVGs—Ambulatory Visit Groups

BBA—Balanced Budget Act (of 1997)
BBRA—Balanced Budget Refinement Act (of 1999)
BIPA—Beneficiary Improvement and Protection Act (of 2000)
BPR—Business Process Reengineering

CA-DRGs—Consolidated Severity-Adjusted DRGs
CAP—Capitated Ambulatory Plan
CBA—Cost Benefit Analysis
CBR—Coding, Billing, and Reimbursement
CBRCO—CBR Compliance Officer
CC (Computer)—Carbon Copy
CC—Coding Clinic
CCI—(CMS's) Correct Coding Initiative
CCO—Chief Compliance Officer
CCR—Cost-to-Charge Ratio
CCs—Complications and Comorbidities
CCU—Critical Care Unit
CDM—Charge Description Master (see generic term "chargemaster")
CENT—Certified Enterostomal Nurse Therapist
CEUs—Continuing Education Units
CF—Conversion Factor
CfC—Conditions for Coverage
CFO—Chief Financial Officer
CfPs—Conditions for Payment (see 42 CFR §424)
CFR—*Code of Federal Regulations*
CHAMPUS—Civilian Health and Medical Program of the Uniformed Services
CHAMPVA—Civilian Health and Medical Program of the Veterans
            Administration
CHC—Community Health Center
CHCP—Coordinated Home Health Program
CIA—Corporate Integrity Agreement (see also Settlement Agreements)
CIO—Chief Information Officer
CIS—Computer Information System
CM—Chargemaster
CMI—Case Mix Index

CMP—Competitive Medical Plan

CMS—Center for Medicare and Medicaid Services

CMS-1450—UB-04 Claim Form as used by Medicare

CMS-1500—1500 Claim Form as used by Medicare

CMS-855—Form used to gain billing privileges for Medicare

CNP—Certified Nurse Practitioner

CNS—Clinical Nurse Specialist

CON—Certificate of Need

COO—Chief Operating Officer

CoPs—Conditions of Participations (see 42 CFR §482; CAHs—42 CFR
    Section 485.600)

CP—Clinical Psychologist

CPT—Current Procedural Terminology (currently CPT-4, anticipated to go to
    CPT-5)

CQI—Continuous Quality Improvement

CRNA—Certified Registered Nurse Anesthetist

CSF—Critical Success Factor

CSW—Clinical Social Worker

CT—Computer Tomographic

CWF—Common Working File

DBMS—Data Base Management System

DED—Dedicated Emergency Department (see EMTALA)

DHHS—Department of Health and Human Services

DME—Durable Medical Equipment

DMEPOS—DME, Prosthetics, Orthotics, Supplies

DMERC—Durable Medical Equipment Regional Carrier (see CMS and both
    MACs)

DNS (Internet)—Domain Name System

DOD—U.S. Department of Defense (see Electronic Shredding Standards)

DOJ—U.S. Department of Justice

DP—Data Processing

DRA—Deficit Reduction Act (of 2005)

DRG—Diagnosis-Related Group(s) (see AP-DRGs, APR-DRGs, SR-DRGs,
    CA-DRGs, MS-DRGs)

EBCDIC (Computer)—Extended Binary Coded Decimal Information Code

ECG—Electrocardiogram

ED—Emergency Department

EDI—Electronic Data Interchange
EEO—Equal Employment Opportunity
EEOC—Equal Employment Opportunity Commission
EGHP—Employer Group Health Plan
EKG—in German, Elektrokardiogramm (see ECG)
E/M—Evaluation and Management
EMC—Electronic Medical Claim
EMG—Electromyography
EMI—Encounter Mix Index
EMTALA—Emergency Medical Treatment and Active Labor Act
EOB—Explanation of Benefits
EOMB—Explanation of Medicare Benefits
EPA—U.S. Environmental Protection Agency
EPCs—Event-Driven Process Chains
EPO—Exclusive Provider Organization
ER—Emergency Room (see also ED, Emergency Department)
ERISA—Employment Retirement Income Security Act
ESRD—End-stage renal disease

FAC—Freestanding Ambulatory Care
FAQs—Frequently Asked Questions
FBI—Federal Bureau of Investigation
FDA—U.S. Food and Drug Administration
FEC—Freestanding Emergency Center
FFS—Fee-for-Service
FFY—Federal Fiscal Year
FI—Fiscal Intermediary
FL—Form Locator (see UB-92)
FLSA—Fair Labor Standards Act
FMR—Focused Medical Review
FMV—Fair Market Value
FQHC—Federally Qualified Health Center
FR—*Federal Register*
FRGs—Functional Related Groups
FRNA—First Registered Nurse Assistant
FTC—Federal Trade Commission
FTP (Internet)—File Transfer Protocol
FY—Fiscal Year

GAF—Geographic Adjustment Factor

GAO—Government Accounting Office

GI—Gastrointestinal

GMLOS—Geometric Mean Length of Stay

GPCI—Geographic Practice Cost Index

GPO—Government Printing Office

GSP—Global Surgical Package

H&P—History and Physical

HCFA—Health Care Financing Administration (now CMS)

HCPCS—Healthcare Common Procedure Coding System (previously HCFA's Common Procedure Coding System)

HFMA—Healthcare Financial Management Association

HHA—Home Health Agency

HHPPS—Home Health Prospective Payment System

HHMCO—Home Health Managed Care Organization

HHS—Health and Human Services

HICN—Health Insurance Claim Number

HIM—Health Information Management (see also Medical Records)

HINNC—Hospital Issued Notice of Noncoverage

HIPAA—Health Insurance Portability and Accountability Act (1996)

HCO—Health Care Organization

HMO—Health Maintenance Organization

HPSA—Health Personnel Shortage Area

HTML—HyperText Markup Language

HTTP (Internet)—HyperText Transfer Protocol

HURA—Health Undeserved Rural Area

HwH—Hospital within a Hospital

I&D—Incision and Drainage

ICD-9-CM—International Classification of Diseases, 9th Revision, Clinical Modification

ICD-10-CM—International Classification of Diseases, 10th Revision, Clinical Modification (replacement for ICD-9-CM Volumes 1 and 2)

ICD-10-PCS—ICD-10 Procedure Coding System (replacement for ICD-9-CM Volume 3)

ICD-11-CM—International Classification of Diseases, 11th Revision, Clinical Modification

ICD-11-PCS—ICD-11 Procedure Coding System
ICU—Intensive Care Unit
IDS—Integrated Delivery System
IG—Inspector General
IOL—Intraocular Lens
IP—Inpatient
IPA—Independent Practice Arrangement/Association
IRS—Internal Revenue Service
IS—Information Systems
ISP—Internet Service Provider
IV—Intravenous

JCAHO—Joint Commission on Accreditation of Healthcare Organizations

KSAPCs—Knowledge, Skills, Abilities, and Personal Characteristics

LCC—Lesser of Costs or Charges
LCD—Local Coverage Decision (see also LMRP)
LMRP—Local Medical Review Policy
LOS—Length of Stay
LTCH—Long-Term Care Hospital
LTRH—Long-Term Rehabilitation Hospital

MAC—Medicare Administrative Contractor
MAC—Monitored Anesthesia Care
MCE—Medicare Code Editor
MCO—Managed Care Organization
MDS—Minimum Data Set
MEI—Medicare Economic Index
MFS—Medicare Fee Schedule
MIS—Management Information System
Modem (Computer)—MODulator-DEModulator
MOG—Medicare Outpatient Grouping
MMA—Medicare Modernization Act (of 2003)
MRI—Magnetic Resonance Imaging
MSA—Metropolitan Statistical Area
MS-DOS (Computer)—Microsoft Disk Operating System
MS-DRGs—Medicare Severity DRGs (CMS established in 2007)
MSOP—Market-Service-Organization-Payment

MSP—Medicare Secondary Payer
MUA—Medically Underserved Area
MUE—Medically Unlikely Edit
MVPS—Medicare Volume Performance Standard

NCD—National Coverage Decision
NCQA—National Committee for Quality Assurance
NCQHC—National Committee for Quality Health Care
NF—Nursing Facility
NONC—Notice of Noncoverage
NP—Nurse Practitioners (some variation; e.g., ARNP—Advanced Registered
    Nurse Practitioner)
NPP—Non-Physician Provider/Practitioner
NM—Nurse Midwife
NSC—National Supplier Clearinghouse
NTIS—National Technical Information Service
NUBC—National Uniform Billing Committee

OASIS—Outcome and Assessment Information Set
OBRA—Omnibus Reconciliation Act
OCE—Outpatient Code Editor
OIG—Office of the Inspector General* (see HHS)
OMB—Office of Management and Budget
OP—Outpatient
OPR—Outpatient Payment Reform
OR—Operating Room
OT—Occupational Therapy or Therapists
OTA—Occupational Therapists Assistant

P&P—Policy and Procedure
PA—Physician Assistant
PAM—Patient Accounts Manager(s)
PBR—Provider-Based Rule (See 42 CFR §413.65)
PECOS—Provider Enrollment, Chain and Ownership System
PERL (Internet)—Practical Extraction and Reporting Language
PET—Positron Emission Tomography
PFS—Patient Financial Services

---

* OIG statistical software available at: http://www.oig.hhs.gov/organization/oas/ratstats.asp

PHO—Physician Hospital Organization
PMPM—Per Member Per Month
POS—Place of Service or Point of Service
PPA—Preferred Provider Arrangement
PPO—Preferred Provider Organization
PPP (Internet)—Point-to-Point Protocol
PPR—Physician Payment Reform
PPS—Prospective Payment System
PRB—Provider Review Board
PRO—Peer Review Organization
ProPAC—Prospective Payment Assessment Commission
PS&E—Provider Statistical and Reimbursement (Report)
PSN—Provider Service Network
PSO—Provider Service Organization
PT—Physical Therapy or Physical Therapist
PTA—Physical Therapy Assistant

QA—Quality Assurance
QFD—Quality Function Deployment

RAPs—Resident Assessment Protocols
RAT-STATS—see OIG Statistical Software
RBRVS—Resource-Based Relative Value System
RC—Revenue Code (see also RCC)
RCC—Revenue Center Codes (from the UB-04 Manual)
RFI—Request for Information
RFP—Request for Proposal
RFQ—Request for Quotation
RHC—Rural Health Clinic
RM—Risk Management
RN—Registered Nurse
RUGs—Resource Utilization Groups
RVS—Relative Value System
RVU—Relative Value Units

SAD—Self-Administrable Drug
S&I—Supervision and Interpretation
SDS—Same-Day Surgery
SGML (Internet)—Standardized General Markup Language

SLP—Speech Language Pathology (see also ST)
SLIP (Internet)—Serial Line IP Protocol
SMI—Service Mix Index
SMTP—Simple Mail Transport Protocol (Internet e-mail)
SNF—Skilled Nursing Facility
SOC—Standard of Care
SR-DRGs—Severity-Refined DRGs (HCFA proposed in 1994)
ST—Speech Therapy (see also SLP)
SUBC—State Uniform Billing Committee

TLAs—Three Letter Acronyms
TPA—Third-Party Administrator
TPP—Third-Party Payer
TQD—Total Quality Deployment
TQM—Total Quality Management
TSC—Transaction Standard/Standard Code Set (see HIPAA)

UB-04—Universal Billing Form-2004 (previously UB-92)
UCR—Usual, Customary, Reasonable
UHC—University Health System Consortium
UHDDS—Uniform Hospital Discharge Data Set
UNIX (Computer)—Not an acronym, but a play on the word "eunuch"
UPIN—Unique Physician Identification Number
UR—Utilization Review
URL—Uniform Resource Locator (Internet Address)
USC—United States Code

VDP—Voluntary Disclosure Program
VSR—Value Stream Reinvention

W-2—Tax Withholding Form
www (Internet)—World Wide Web

XML (Internet)—eXtensible Markup Language

Index

Author

Duane C. Abbey, PhD, CFP, is a management consultant and president of Abbey & Abbey Consultants, Inc. Based in Ames, Iowa, Abbey & Abbey specializes in healthcare consulting and related areas.

Dr. Abbey, whose work in healthcare now spans more than 25 years, earned his graduate degrees at the University of Notre Dame and Iowa State University. Today, he spends about half of his time developing and teaching workshops (for students who affectionately quip that the *Federal Register* is his favorite reading material) and making presentations to professional organizations. He devotes the other half to consulting work that involves performing chargemaster reviews, compliance reviews, providing litigation support, and conducting reimbursement studies.

Dr. Abbey also uses his mathematical and financial background to perform financial assessments, develop complex financial models, and conduct various types of statistical work. His studies in the field of neurolinguistic programming have enhanced his ability to provide organizational communication facilitation services for healthcare organizations. He also provides litigation support services for attorneys representing healthcare providers in legal proceedings.

Dr. Abbey can be contacted by e-mail at Duane@aaciweb.com.

Printed in the United States
by Baker & Taylor Publisher Services